D1568074

FOUNTAIN PENS

Series editor: Frédérique Crestin-Billet
Design: Lélie Carnot
Color separation by Chesteroc Graphics
Translated from the French by David Radzinowicz
Originally published as La Folle des Stylos à Plume
© 2001 Flammarion, Paris
English-language edition © 2002 Flammarion USA Inc.

ISBN: 2-0801-0719-4
Printed in France

Collectible
FOUNTAIN
PENS

Juan Manuel Clark

Flammarion

That love letter, those profoundly faithful or deeply sincere sign-offs, those words of tenderness, those promises and secrets— are you really going to bang them out on a computer keyboard? Where's your Montblanc, where's your Conway Stewart, to put to paper, not just ink but something more than mere words? Surely your heartfelt sentiments, your soulful confessions, your romantic outpourings can only be adequately expressed with the aid of a real fountain pen?—A gold one if possible, though steel will do too. A fountain pen, perfectly balanced in the hand, will allow you to formulate your ideas more clearly—even if just now you have no idea what you're going to say...

CONTENTS

Introduction

Webster's Dictionary defines writing as "the act or art of forming letters and characters on paper, wood, stone, or other material, for the purpose of recording the ideas which characters and words express, or of communicating them to others by visible signs." Writing, which evolved at different times and in different places around the world, is what made history possible. Yet without delving too deeply into the stupendous story of writing, it is worth noting that for 40,000 of the 50,000 years since *Homo sapiens* has been *sapiens* (that is, since humankind has been aware of its own knowledge) it got by without writing, the first traces of the written word dating to only 5,500 years ago.

O nce writing was invented, the media on which its signs were inscribed soon began to evolve too, and, in their wake, the implements that were used to write them down. The first great leap forward is owed to the Egyptians, who came up with a lightweight and resistant writing surface known to us as papyrus. Using sharpened calamus reeds, whose fibers were capable of retaining an ink composed of water and soot-black, they covered sheets of papyrus in hieroglyphics. Then, around the year 200 B.C.E., Eumenius II, king of Pergamon, dreamt up the idea of building the largest library in the world. To scupper his ambition, the king of Egypt is supposed to have denied Eumenius all access to papyrus. It's an ill wind, however, and this setback served as a spur to the invention of smooth, white, two-sided parchment made out of

Metal Roman styli were used on wax-coated wooden tablets. In spite of first papyrus, then parchment, and lastly paper, this ancient medium continued in use up to the Middle Ages. One wrote with the point, the flattened face being employed for rubbing out. Like goose quills, such objects are the ancestors of the metal pen.

animal hide. Although this is only a hypo-
thesis, it is thought that the appearance of
parchment was linked to that of the goose
quill: calamus was well adapted to the rough surface of papyrus, but the quill was better suited to
soft parchment or vellum. The arrival of paper, a
Chinese invention of around 105 C.E., did not,
however, render obsolete the use of the
quill. Paper was made from a pulp composed of various plants (among which,
mulberry and bamboo), rags and hemp.
Production techniques emigrated to
Europe via Asia Minor, the first factory
being established in Javita, Spain, in
1154. Paper spread rapidly throughout
Europe, thanks to its low cost
and the ease with which manu-
factories could be set up.
Now that it was so readily available, paper was the perfect material on which to print books

(Gutenberg issued his first Bible in 1457), and the publication of printed material led to an increase in literacy. This in turn resulted in an increased demand for quills, for not only did more people than ever before want to read the printed word, they also wanted to put pen to paper. Geese were not the only birds to sacrifice their flight feathers to further the written word: crows, turkeys, and ducks were all commandeered for the purpose.

Until the end of the nineteenth century, the consumption of quills was such that, in England, gaggles of the birds were farmed solely to provide writing instruments. The operation did not consist, however, in pelting after a passing goose and, in a cloud of dust and down, grabbing a feather or two from her behind before dunking it without further ado into a pot of ink. No, preparing a quill for use as a pen called for skill: first, it was necessary to remove the fat since it renders the ink useless. This was done by dipping the feathers into a preheated sand bath and then wiping them spotlessly clean. Then the quills had to be meticulously

For centuries, be it for love letters, commercial correspondence, religious, philosophical, or scientific texts, the commonest writing implement was the quill. Its supremacy lasted from the early Middle Ages to the nineteenth century: a decent innings for a humble tool!

trimmed, not only at the point that was to be dipped into the ink, but also at the opposite end, which had to be considerably short-ened. The long, majestic quills one sees in swashbuckling movies are thus more myth than reality. Moreover, since the writing point was apt to blunt quickly, the tip had to be regularly trimmed and shaped with a "pen knife". The most sophisticated models of these specialized tools incorporated upwards of six blades to ensure that at least one of them remained sharp.

Many attempts were made to fit quills with an ink reservoir to reduce the number of times that the hand had to travel back and forth between paper and inkhorn. Countless systems were devised, the most worthwhile being the double quill fitted with an inner duct serving as a reservoir. In 1809, a British manufacturer, Joseph Bramah, developed a process for making pre-trimmed goose quill sec-tions that could be mounted on the pen-holder and held in place by a locking ring. This invention reduced manufacturing costs considerably, since a number of writing quills could be cut from a single flight feather. Success was immediate and lasted until the metal nib finally supplanted the long-lived goose quill.

Eighteenth-century goose quills with storage case. These quills have most probably been used in the past and one can see that these functional tools are very different in appearance from those seen in many paintings and engravings. Though it is now defunct, it was thanks to the quill that Western calligraphy earned its spurs!

The metal nib began to become popular around 1845–50, but it was not a wholly novel piece of hardware. Several authorities cite references dating back to the fifteenth century, particularly for brass nibs, and it should not be forgotten that metal had already been used in the stylus of medieval and Roman times. Fine gold pen-holders from the seventeenth and eighteenth centuries have also come down to us. What was new in the middle of the nineteenth century, however, was that the pen

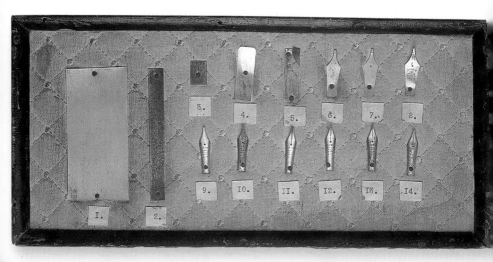

became a mass-produced article that was soon made available to a large number of consumers. In England, at the time the greatest industrial power in Europe, fortunes were made from the metal dip-pen, an instrument that continued scribbling away in school exercise books until at least 1960. But steel is not gold. Although the noble metal offers unrivaled suppleness of hand, its major shortcoming lies in its rapid rate of wear. Once more it was two British inventors, Doughty and Rose, who made it possible to extend the lifetimes of gold nibs by fitting them with a ruby point. There's no stopping progress, however, and, thanks to the discoveries of William Hyde Woolaston, ruby was ousted around 1834 by iridium, a fantastically hard-wearing metal.

A superb solid-gold and tortoiseshell example of the pen invented by Rose and made by Doughty: the top of the nib is shown in close-up above.
Opposite: the various stages in the assembly of metal nibs, from cutting the steel to tipping the point with iridium.

Goose quill or steel nib?

Writers down the years have expressed strong preferences with regard to the tools of their trade. In Poetry and Truth, Goethe says that he preferred to write solely in pencil and railed against quill pens whose endless scratching interfered with the flow of his inspiration. For his part,

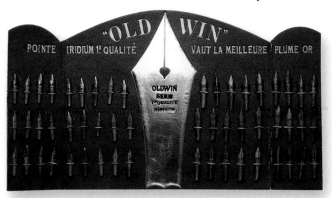

Alexandre Dumas is said to have consumed thousands of goose quills in the course of writing his mammoth novels, in spite of there being perfectly adequate steel nibs available at the time. And Rudyard Kipling affectionately describes in his memoirs a thin eight-sided pen made of agate, another of silver in the form of a quill and a smooth black pen made in Jerusalem. A great fan of Japanese art, he also loved his lacquered Namiki (page 238).

*The first
English patent lodged by
Frederick Fölsch in May 1809 included a
notable innovation: a spring-loaded plunger that expels
ink from reservoir to nib.*

I t was the marketing of large numbers of hard-wearing nibs that did the most to further the invention and development of what were called at the time "reservoir pens" and what we call today "fountain pens." This change in terminology has a technological basis, however: earlier models had only an ink reservoir, whereas true fountain pens incorporate a system that guarantees a regular supply of ink to the nib.

The Penographic
*or "Self-Filling Writing Instrument"
patented by the Englishman John Scheffer in 1819. The button
on the side squeezed ink from an inner reservoir down to the nib.*

This pen was developed by John Jacob Parker in 1832 (not to be confused with the American George Parker). The reservoir was filled with the aid of piston, as against a number of rival models, for example that by Scheffer presented on the previous page. This extremely rare example is one of the first made.

Its development was quite a headache, however, and it proved to be a puzzle that preoccupied hundreds of inventors throughout the nineteenth century. Be they English, French, or Italian, an impressive number of patents were lodged, initially in Europe. Many names have been forgotten, and many prototypes have vanished—but the sheer mass of patents witnesses to the amount of brain power that was brought to bear on the problem. Some of these inventors have earned their place in history, however, among them Frenchman Jean-Benoît Mallat, who invented the *Siphoïde* in 1884. It wasn't exactly a fountain pen, however, since the ink feed had some way to progress, but at

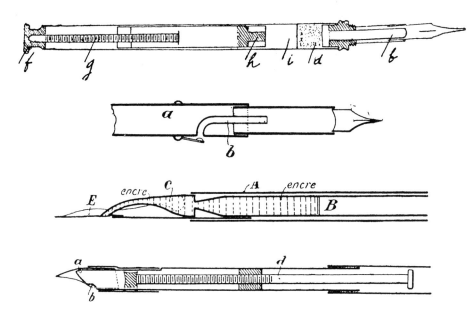

From top to bottom: patents by Victor Legendre (1836), Reeb and Séjourné, pharmacy assistants at Strasbourg hospital (1852), Noël (1853), Simon de Vaudiville, stenographer at the French National Assembly (1860), all quite forgotten today. Like those lodged by Michel Hommel, Henri Farjas, and like Laffont's Capillographe, they demonstrate the period's immense ingenuity, which found an outlet, moreover, in the design not only of fountain pens but also of any number of everyday objects, such as pocket knives, corkscrews, watches, pipes, etc.

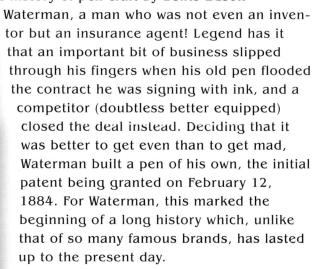

least this range could be mass-produced and it met with a measure of commercial success. The definitive solution came from America, with the development of the first reliable ink duct in the history of pen craft by Lewis Edson Waterman, a man who was not even an inventor but an insurance agent! Legend has it that an important bit of business slipped through his fingers when his old pen flooded the contract he was signing with ink, and a competitor (doubtless better equipped) closed the deal instead. Deciding that it was better to get even than to get mad, Waterman built a pen of his own, the initial patent being granted on February 12, 1884. For Waterman, this marked the beginning of a long history which, unlike that of so many famous brands, has lasted up to the present day.

The Ink Bottle

Ink was originally made using soot-black, and in the age of the quill pen its flow characteristics had much improved. It was produced from various vegetable tannins mixed with iron sulfate. By the time metal nibs made their appearance, inks were chemical products that could be synthesized in all sorts of colors. In the 1920s, pen companies began marketing their own brands of ink. It was not that they were radically different from one another, just that bottle and box were handy for publicizing trademarks. The first ink to be dedicated to a particular pen line was Qulnk (contraction of Quick Ink), which followed the launch of the Parker 51 in 1941. It would be truer to say that the ink existed first, the pen being designed to make the most of its quick-drying properties.

ENCRE
SPÉCIALE
POUR
LOGRAPHE

A very fine pen with its own teat pipette or "eye-dropper," an early filling system that producers strove to make less messy and more practical in succeeding years.

The age of the fountain pen really kicked off at the end of the 1880s. Once the nib had been perfected, the ink made more free-flowing and purified, the main points of proper functioning understood, it only remained to refine the product, improve the performance and efficiency, and the reduce price.

As regards this last point, an important role was played by ebonite (see page 56). Compared with silver and gold, low-cost models could be mass-produced, though this did not stem the manufacture of luxury lines.

A "correspondence bureau" at the firm of Mercier Champagne in 1908. It can be seen that the market for writing instruments was far from insignificant!

As will be shown in the following pages, most of the technical innovations and refinements in the years up to the 1930s centered around the mechanism that acted as the filling system for the fountain pen. After that time, producers were more or less entirely preoccupied with aesthetic considerations, and all the more after the arrival of celluloid had made it easier to produce pens in diverse shapes and colors. The history of the fountain pen is also a business conflict whose key battles took place essentially on the American continent, the main contenders being Waterman, Parker, Sheaffer, and Wahl Eversharp. These companies were soon exporting their pens to Europe, and two of them —Parker and Waterman— were subsequently to

"SWAN" FOUNTPENS

owe their survival respectively to their French and British subsidiaries. Other American and European manufacturers occasionally came up with fruitful ideas too, but not on the same scale as that enjoyed by the dominant "four majors" of that time.

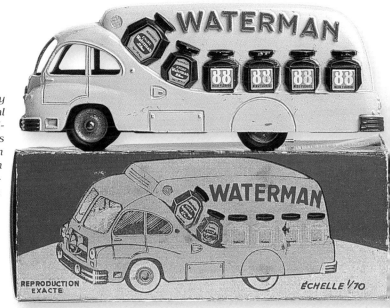

Apart naturally from technical and aesthetic criteria, the success of a make of pen depended too on advertising campaigns for which no stone was left unturned...

Significant Dates

Below are some key dates in the history of fountain pens and their manufacturers.

1813: *Jean De La Rue begins business in London.*
1841: *John Holland founds his firm at Cincinnati, Ohio.*
1842: *Jean-Benoît Mallat sets up the company in France that bears his name.*
1847: *Maison Cartier founded.*
1856: *Creation of the Eagle Pencil and Pen Company in the United States.*
1864: *Aikin Lambert established in New York.*
1872: *Simon Tissot-Dupont founds the Société Dupont in Paris.*
1873: *Mabie, Todd & Bard established in New York.*
1875: *Soennecken set up in Germany.*
1877: *Alonzo Townsend Cross begins trading.*
1878: *Paul Wirt sets up his business in Bloomsburg, Pennsylvania, while in Europe Günther Wagner registers the Pelikan brand name.*
1882: *Waterman Ideal Fountain Pen created in New York.*
1888: *Parker Pen Co. founded.*
1894: *Creation of the English subsidiary of Mabie Todd, famous for its Swan pens.*
1896: *Beginnings of the Moore Pen Company.*
1898: *Roy Conklin establishes the Conklin Pen Company at Toledo, Ohio.*
1905: *Creation of Conway Stewart in London.*
1906: *Creation in Hamburg of what will become the Montblanc trademark.*
1907: *Alfred Dunhill founds Dunhill in London.*
1911: *Creation of Sailor, near Hiroshima, Japan.*

1911: Foundation of Elmo that will later become Montegrappa.
1913: Walter Sheaffer and his associates found the Sheaffer Pen Company.
1916: The firm that will become La Plume d'Or is established.
1917: Foundation of Wahl Eversharp.
1918: Creation of Namiki that will become Pilot; and foundation of Le Bœuf, at Springfield, Massachusetts.
1919: Creation of Auror at Turin; Gold Starry begins production in France; foundation of Osmia in Germany and of Unic in Paris.
1925: Armand Simoni sets up the firm of Osma at Bologna.
1926: Jules Fagard founds Jif Waterman in Paris.
1930: Lamy established in Heidelberg, Germany.
1932: Aikin Lambert merges with Waterman.
1933: Le Bœuf collapses.
1934: The Bayard trademark appears in France.
1937: Wirt ceases trading.
1947: Conklin's concern folds.
1956: Moore ceases business activity.
1957: Conway Stewart ceases trading; Eversharp bought out by Parker, only to disappear shortly afterwards.
1958: In London, De La Rue fails.
1967: The German firm Soennecken closes for business.
1971: Under the aegis of Francine Gomez, Waterman becomes French.
1973: The Italian firm Stipula set up.
1987: Waterman bought out by the American Gillette group.
1988: Foundation of the Italian company Visconti.
1990s: Several great names are reborn: Eversharp (unsuccessfully), Conway Stewart, Conklin, Le Bœuf... It is still too early to say what the future holds in store for them.

P en collecting comes in any number of guises: there's the purely technical interest, where the aim is to acquire every system whether or not it succeeded in living up to expectations; then there's the aesthetic aspect; and then the methodical accumulation of little known lines or no-name pens. Whichever is your favored approach, it will always depend, to a considerable extent, on the financial means at your disposal.

It should be stressed that in the last few years something of a renaissance in the fountain pen world has taken place, and it may be that it will soon be entering a second golden age. Perhaps the moment has therefore come to buy up all and everything, including recent and cheaper lines, and leave the weeding out until later. Whatever the future holds, the world of the pen is a fascinating one, and even if an exhaustive collection is not your goal you'll find much in this book to whet your curiosity about an instrument that has for so long served to transmit our thoughts, our culture, and our ideas...

André Mora is one of the foremost authorities on the historic fountain pen. Collectors the world over turn to him for advice about purchases and for repairs of every kind that he himself, thanks to his vast stock of spare parts, is pleased to undertake. Of course he also sells modern pens.

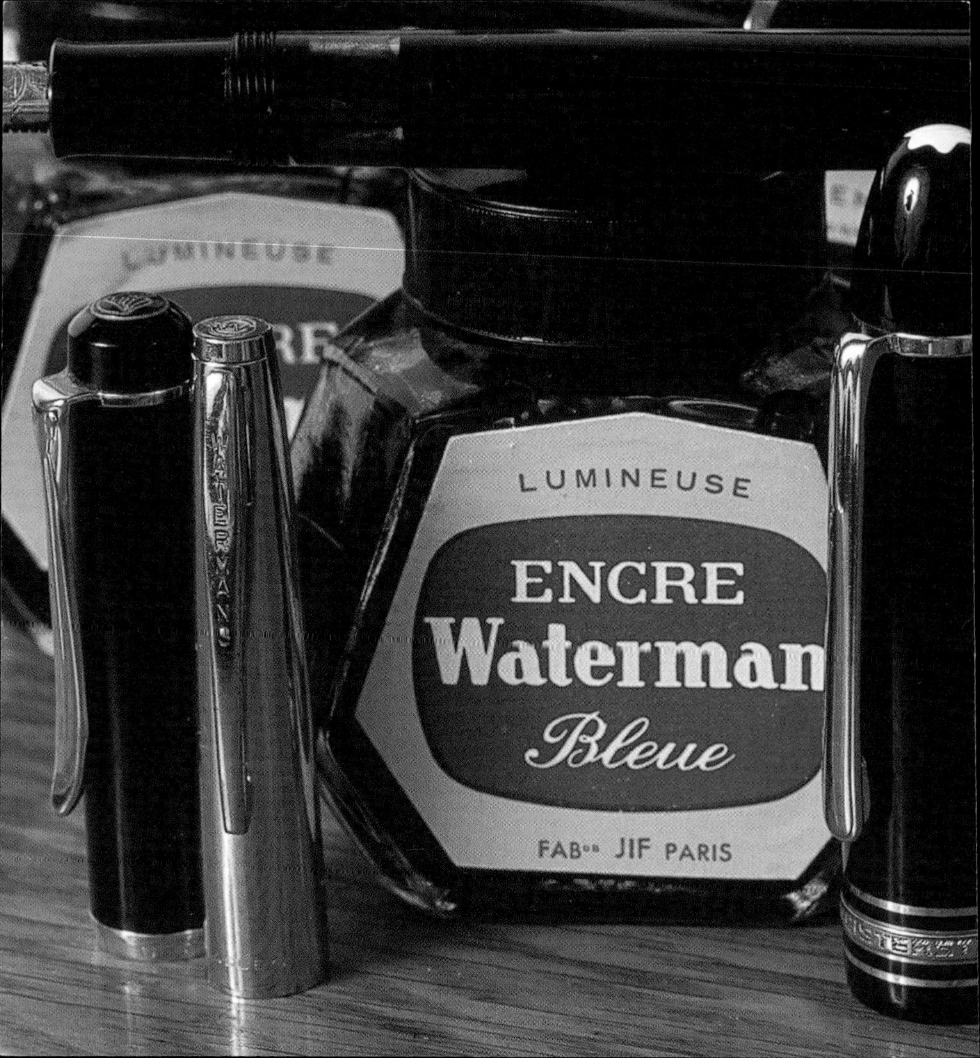
LUMINEUSE
ENCRE
Waterman
Bleue
FABᵒᴮ JIF PARIS
WATERMAN'S

I

VINTAGE
fountain pens

E ver since the end of the nineteenth century, when the first genuine fountain pen models were created, right up until the 1930s, by which time all the filling systems had been perfected, the history of the pen has been a running battle between the major American manufacturers. A great number of models might never have been designed and manufactured were it not for the need to produce an "answer" to a pen that a competitor had just brought out. As the dust settled, other makers, some of them based on the European continent, also came up with new ideas and captured their share of the market.

These two models are in fact more pen-holders with a reservoir than genuine fountain pens, since the ink channel lacks one essential feature: the thin grooves that allow the ink to be drawn down by capillary action, hence ensuring a regular supply. This is a Monographe whose patent was granted in 1889 to Jules-Michel and Jean-Émile Rubin, Jean Falconnet, and Joseph Sautier.

The Klio, made by the German firm Werk Hennef, dates from the 1900s. To procure one for yourself, you simply had to slip a 50-cent piece in a fold in one of the company's cards and send it off to the distributor in New York, the Spencerian Pen Co., who would then ship you a pen by return of post. This line met with considerable success at the time.

"KLIO"
INK-CONTROLLED FOUNTAIN PEN
ADAPTED FOR SPENCERIAN PENS.

KLIO

PECULIARITIES

1. Ink will not flow out on the points when held downward.
2. **Ink cannot be shaken out.**
3. The flow of ink is controlled by the fingers when writing.
4. Any excess of ink can be drawn back from the pen into the holder.
5. No joint from which ink can leak on the fingers when writing.
6. The only first-class Fountain Pen for steel pens, so that

ADVANTAGES

carried in the pocket, in any posi-
the clothing.
2. **No nee** surplus ink on the floor or desk
3. Fresh pens can be inser an ordinary holder.
4. Can be used with any pen, steel or gold, that suits the handwriting

To SPENCERIAN PEN CO., New York City.

Enclosed in this card you will find 50 cents for one "KLIO" FOUNTAIN PEN. Please send promptly post paid.

Name

Town

Street

State

Lewis Edson Waterman's beginnings in the pen world date from 1883. The model illustrated here is from 1894. As well as a circular "eye," the nib also possesses a horseshoe feature. This type of nib continued in use between 1891 and 1894.

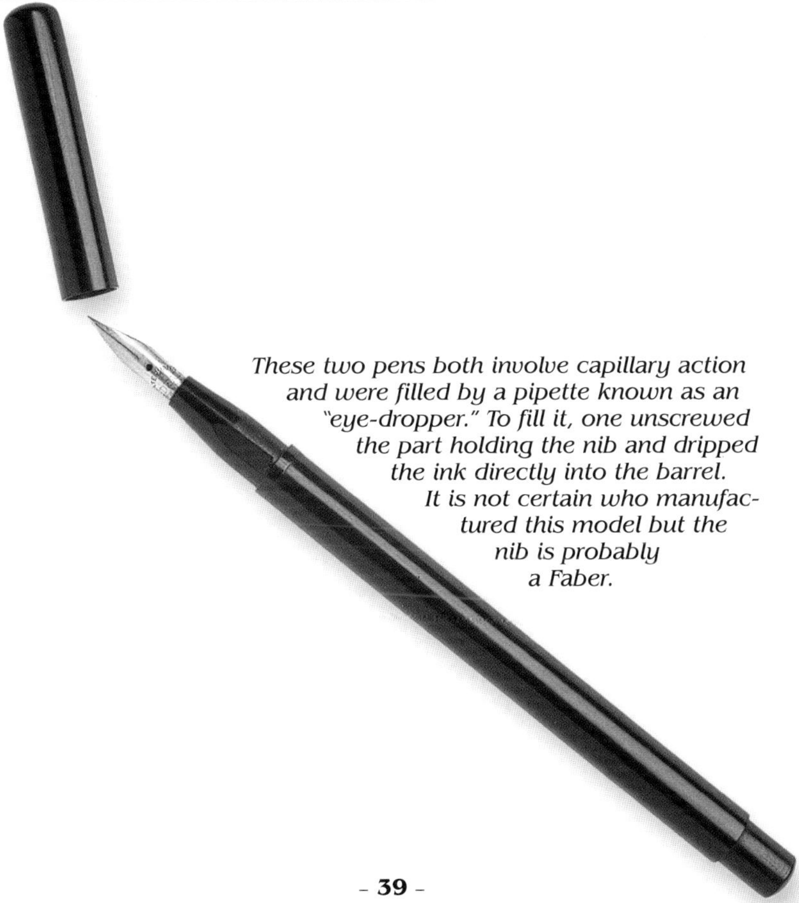

These two pens both involve capillary action and were filled by a pipette known as an "eye-dropper." To fill it, one unscrewed the part holding the nib and dripped the ink directly into the barrel. It is not certain who manufactured this model but the nib is probably a Faber.

In 1894, George Saford Parker invented the "lucky curve," an ink-delivery system with a knee-bend feed that allows the ink to flow into the reservoir, ensuring that no droplets gather by the time the pen is opened. When the pen is placed nip upwards, ink drains naturally into the sac. A small quantity, however, remains ready in the capillary channel. Unfortunately, the warmth of the hand increased the pressure inside the pen and when the cap was removed, the build-up caused the ink to be expelled, spattering the fingers in the process.

*This Parker No. 1
lucky curve dates from
1898, a date at which an "overfeed" nib was still the norm; later, this
was superseded by "underfeed" models. For
a collector to unearth such a pen, and in a perfect
state of conservation and complete with its original
box and instruction leaflet, constitutes a real find
(see also page 69).*

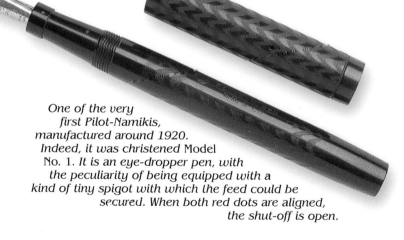

*One of the very
first Pilot-Namikis,
manufactured around 1920.
Indeed, it was christened Model
No. 1. It is an eye-dropper pen, with
the peculiarity of being equipped with a
kind of tiny spigot with which the feed could be
secured. When both red dots are aligned,
the shut-off is open.*

This is a Pelican—not to be confused with the German company Pelikan. In 1895, the first pens produced by De La Rue, an English company specializing in color printing, were marketed under this name. A large company, De La Rue held a monopoly over postage-stamp printing in Great Britain.

In 1890, the
Eagle Pencil Company had been
the first to market a filling arrange-
ment involving little tubes of glass, or
"vials." Although the system represents
the height of ingenuity, the cartridges
were needless to say incredibly fragile. The
principle was abandoned, only to resurface
many decades later with,
as everyone knows, far greater success.
The present model dates from 1898.

This pump-filler pen is a 1920s Waterman. The transparent body, a feature that eventually became popular with all suppliers, is made of Bakelite.

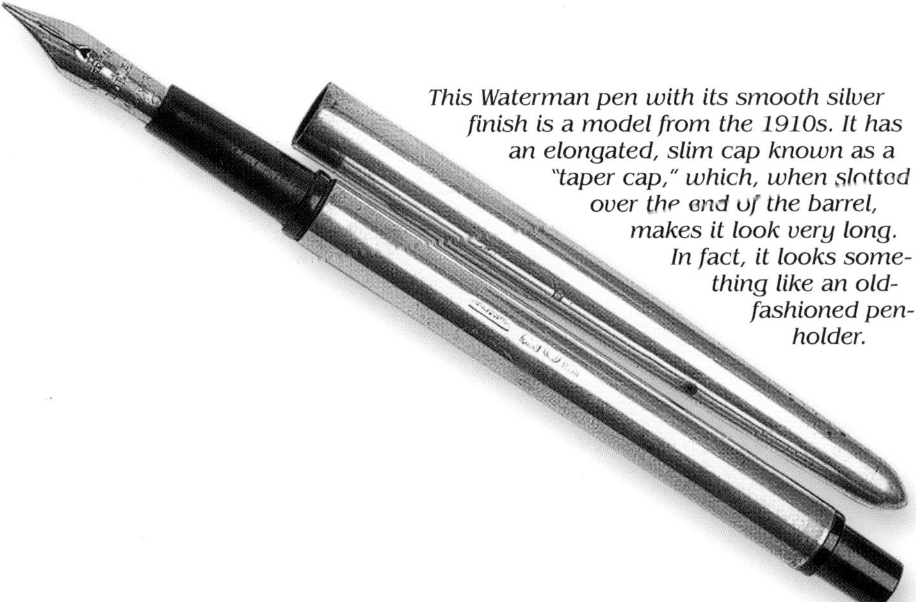

This Waterman pen with its smooth silver
finish is a model from the 1910s. It has
an elongated, slim cap known as a
"taper cap," which, when slotted
over the end of the barrel,
makes it look very long.
In fact, it looks some-
thing like an old-
fashioned pen-
holder.

The Aikin Lambert Pen Company began trading in 1864 in New York. Initially a nib manufacturer, it began making pens in the 1890s. Its models were always very attractive, as shown by the present example from the 1920s. Aikin Lambert merged with Waterman in 1932 and was responsible for many of the latter company's cases, so that lines by the two firms are often difficult to tell apart.

As with
the example on
page 45, this Camel
model made by Dunn Pen is
a see-through. Note the large size
of the barrel, a characteristic typical
of early piston fillers. This one dates
from 1921, the year the firm was set
up. The business didn't last for long,
however, as it shut up shop in 1924.
Dunn also produced a model called
the Dreadnought.

In 1897, Roy Conklin invented the "magic crescent": pressure on the disk collapsed a rubber bladder which then sucked up the ink, while a special locking ring prevented the sac from expelling ink when accidentally compressed. This crescent dates from 1901 and is one of the rare gold-plated models, black ebonite being far commoner (see page 87).

Morris W. Moore applied for a patent for a retractable nib in 1896. Marketed a few years later, the
system protects the point when it is not in use.
Fully extended, the nib blocks off the ink flow from
the chamber, hence its name, "safety." Retracted, it
allows access to the reservoir, the pen being filled
with an eye-dropper. The gold-plated model
comes from before the 1920s.

Dating from 1905, this safety pen was made by Caw's Pen and Ink Co., which ceased trading ten years after this model was released. To extend the nib, one has to insert and turn the screw cap at the end of the pen; this prevents one damaging the point by accidentally forgetting to retract it before capping.

These two retractable
pens by Waterman date
from the 1920s. When the nut at
the end of the barrel is turned, the
spiral retractor activates a rod that
slides along two grooves in the body.
Filling is only possible when the nib is housed,
but care is called for since there is no mechanism
to stop the ink from running out when the pen is
inverted. A device in the cap, though, prevents this even-
tuality when the pen is capped.

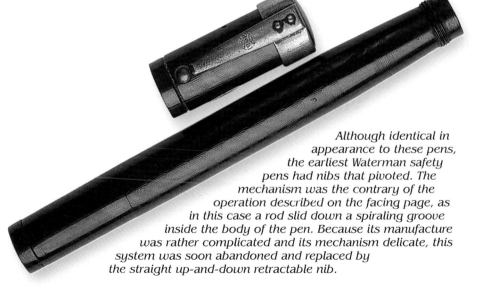

Although identical in appearance to these pens, the earliest Waterman safety pens had nibs that pivoted. The mechanism was the contrary of the operation described on the facing page, as in this case a rod slid down a spiraling groove inside the body of the pen. Because its manufacture was rather complicated and its mechanism delicate, this system was soon abandoned and replaced by the straight up-and-down retractable nib.

*Safety pens
enjoyed a flourish-
ing success in Europe
that continued right up until the
outbreak of the Second World War.
This model dates from 1925, the year
in which the Italian firm of Omas was
founded. The name is an acronym for
Officina Meccanica Armando Simoni, a company that initially specialized in the production of precision spare parts.*

Before becoming Montblanc, the little company that manufactured retractable Rouge et Noir pens—so dubbed for their color scheme— was called the Simplo Filler Pen Co., founded in Hamburg in 1908. This gold-plated Safety No. 1 comes from 1922, a date at which the name Montblanc was already being employed for other products, red and black models continuing to be known as Rouge et Noir.

A few years after vulcanized rubber had been invented by Charles Goodyear in 1839, the Englishman Thomas Hancock christened the material "ebonite" and developed reliable techniques for its industrial production. The advantages of hard rubber include low cost, impermeability, and resistance to the corrosion occasioned by ink, while in addition it is relatively easy to work on a lathe. On the other hand, rounded and tapered forms are diffi-cult to produce and the colors are hardly very varied, being limited to black, red, and two-tone, as in this "mottled" Waterman 12, from the 1910s.

Prior to the arrival of celluloid—that is, to the end of the 1920s—hard rubber was the preferred material for pens. To try to make the material more attractive, it was occasionally engraved: this is a so-called "chased" model, a 20, from 1915. It is the largest of all Waterman pens: the same exists in pure red and in red and black "marble" ebonite.

The J. G. Rider Pen Company was founded in 1905 in Illinois, only to vanish without trace twenty years later. The cap clip, in addition to its usual function, was used to extend the exceptionally long feed tube by way of a small pin. Once pulled out the pen was filled with an eye dropper. This hard rubber model dates from 1910–15.

"The word 'Stylomine' is not in the dictionary—it's a registered trademark": so ran the advertising for this French company. And indeed, Zuber, which manufactured nibs, clips, and other components, succeeded in registering the name in 1921. It was only in 1925, though, that the first fountain pens, such as this safety, eventually came out. It is of a quality and inventiveness that is the exception rather than the rule in the French industry at that time, and Stylomine was soon making a name for itself with other products (see page 158).

To brighten up the ebonite bodies and increase the value of the pen, between around 1900 and 1925 many manufacturers introduced so-called filigree cases. In fact this is not true "filigree" work, but cut metal. Page 247 shows an illustration of a piece with real metal filigree.

Much sought after, filigree work extended to many types of pen and cases. The names of the makers of all these are unknown. They date from 1915, except for the top one on the facing page, which is older. Note too its visible "overfeed" nib. This system, which was the equal of underfeed in terms of performance, was abandoned for purely aesthetic reasons.

Three filigree pens by Waterman, dating from 1910. The slenderest is a 412½. According to the manufacturer's numbering system, the "½" indicates a model slimmer than standard. The oldest Waterman filigree known is a long, thin "taper cap," from 1898.

Two more superb Waterman filigrees, from 1920, one silver and the other gold. Stubbier than average, and incorporating a ring cap, these are probably ladies' models. The ring can be threaded with a ribbon or a thin chain to turn the pen into a pendant. Note the fine initials in an Art Deco style of lettering.

This superb red hard rub-
ber 1910 Waterman, quite
apart from its silver filigree
work (rarer than over black), is
also a safety. This type of pen
can be identified immediately
by its cap, which is somewhat
stunted compared with pens
equipped with other systems.

In a bid to counter Conklin's immense success with the crescent filler (page 49), in 1913 Waterman launched its "coin filler," the coin being a special disk presented with the pen on purchase that is pressed down on a metal pressure bar which then squeezes the rubber sac. The model is extremely rare today, since its lack of success meant it was produced for just one year. To find one with filigree work is real turn-up for the book!

The coin filler was available in two lines, the pocket self filler (PSF) and the vest pocket (VP), like this one, designed with the waistcoat in mind. The coin could be hung from the clip— though it that case the pen couldn't be fixed onto the pocket—or else atta- ched to a match- chain.

The jeweler Walter Sheaffer, finding all existing filling systems old-fashioned, cobbled together his own, and so created the first genuine lever fountain pen (one of the original models is shown on page 223). The one here, with its squared-off lines, is a 1920 Lifetime. It was a luxury item at the time and owed much of its success to the lifetime guarantee that it carried.

*After the failure of the coin filler,
Waterman too ended up adopting the
lever system. To avoid falling foul of
Sheaffer's patent, Waterman acquired an
earlier one granted to a certain Barnes. In
fact, this system was superior even to
Sheaffer's, since, rather than being
set directly into the barrel, the
lever was housed in a box section, as can be seen here.
This model from the
1920s is special in
being trimmed with
two gold bands.*

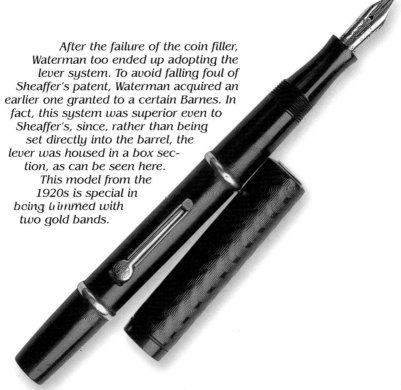

This 1920 Parker is a lucky curve. It is infrequent to find this type of model in an untouched state, since many repairers would section the feed "curve" (see page 41), so releasing it and making it easier to mend the pen.

Once the basic technical innovations became generally adopted, Parker concentrated on color to keep sales buoyant in a sector that was heading for a slump. Taking up an idea of one of its employees, Lewis Tebbel, in 1921 the firm reissued a pre-existing model, the Jackknife, but in bright orange hard rubber: the Duofold. The really clever idea, however, was to sell the pen at what was, for the time, the relatively high price of 7 dollars, so making it into a symbol of education in an America that remained fifty per cent illiterate. This example is exceptional in its pristine state and in coming with its original price sticker.

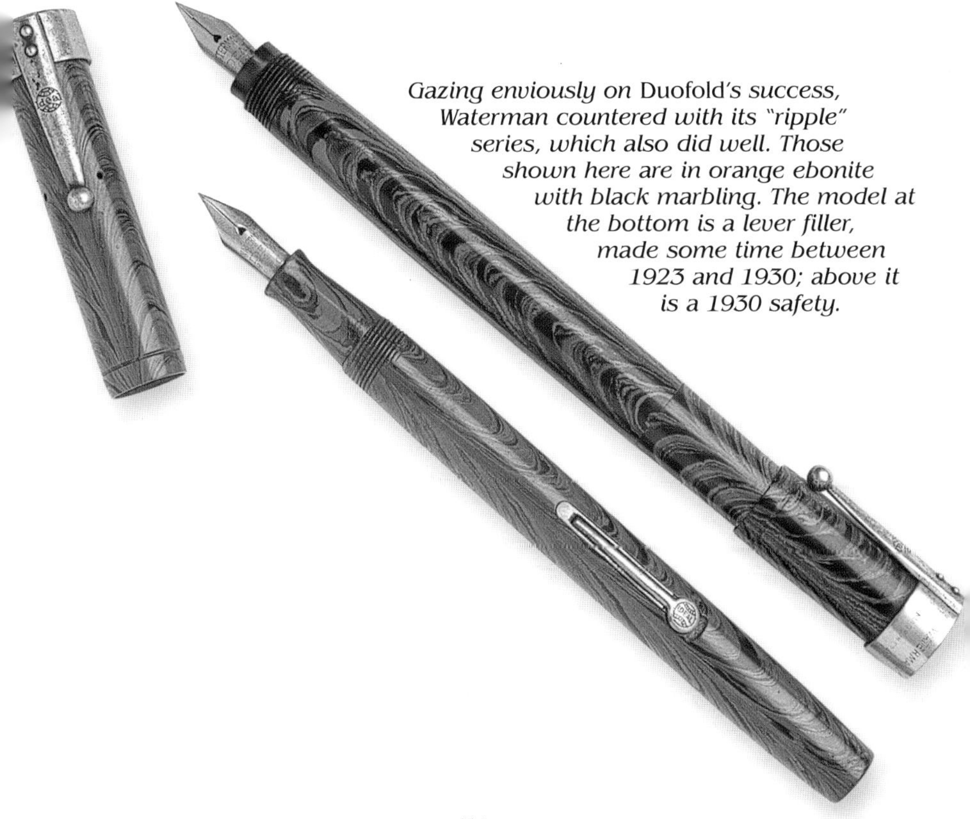

Gazing enviously on Duofold's success, Waterman countered with its "ripple" series, which also did well. Those shown here are in orange ebonite with black marbling. The model at the bottom is a lever filler, made some time between 1923 and 1930; above it is a 1930 safety.

Although in hindsight it is easy to see that hard rubber was in general decline in industrial applications, Waterman persisted in worthy attempts to introduce variety in its lines by coloring the material. Shown here are Ripples in olive, blue and...

pink flavors. Over time, these pens have acquired a kind of patina that is most attractive to collectors, but at the time they seemed rather dull compared with the celluloid models that Sheaffer had already been marketing for two years. Coloring ebon- ite also rendered the pens more fragile.

Still, Waterman did not stop there. As if for some fountain pen parlor game, it issued Ripples with cap bands in different colors, each indicating a different grade of nib: the pink is a flexible fine for shorthand; the red, a standard nib for general use; the yellow, rounded for rapid writing; the green, rigid for carbon copies, and so on...

*To these colors can be added
purple, blue, and black and, in point
of fact, two more, gray and brown.
Depending on the markets concerned,
these last two replaced purple whose nib was
suited to oblique hands. These models were
available in two sizes: No. 7, originally sold at
7 dollars, and the smaller No. 5, sold for 5.*

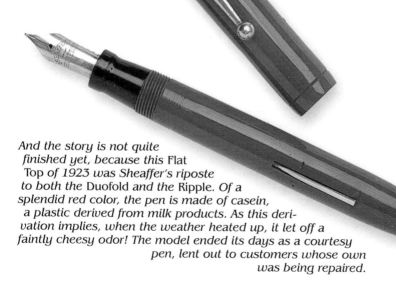

And the story is not quite
finished yet, because this Flat
Top of 1923 was Sheaffer's riposte
to both the Duofold and the Ripple. Of a
splendid red color, the pen is made of casein,
a plastic derived from milk products. As this deri-
vation implies, when the weather heated up, it let off a
faintly cheesy odor! The model ended its days as a courtesy
pen, lent out to customers whose own
was being repaired.

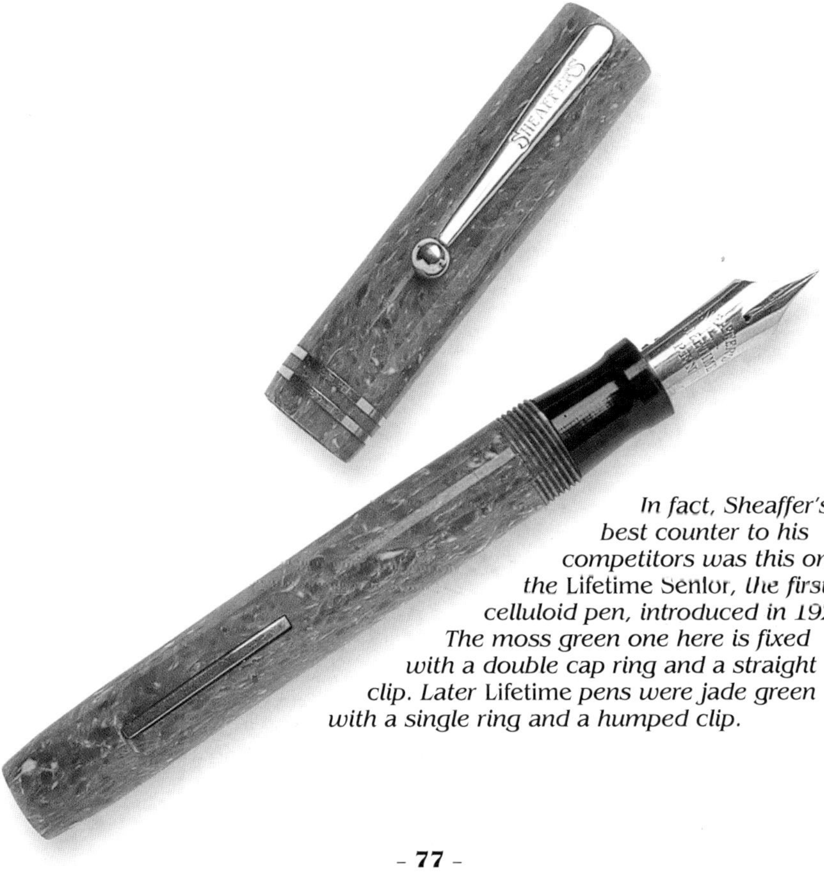

In fact, Sheaffer's best counter to his competitors was this one: the Lifetime Senior, the first celluloid pen, introduced in 1924. The moss green one here is fixed with a double cap ring and a straight clip. Later Lifetime pens were jade green with a single ring and a humped clip.

Christened Permanite by Parker, Radite by Sheaffer,
and Pyraline by other makers, the material that
introduced a really wide range of colors to the
pen world was one and the same—celluloid.
This is one of Parker's first plastic pens,
dating from 1926. In fact, it is a fore-
runner of the Duofold, but the presti-
gious name is not in evidence:
the material was still proving
unstable at this stage and
the company was
taking no risks!

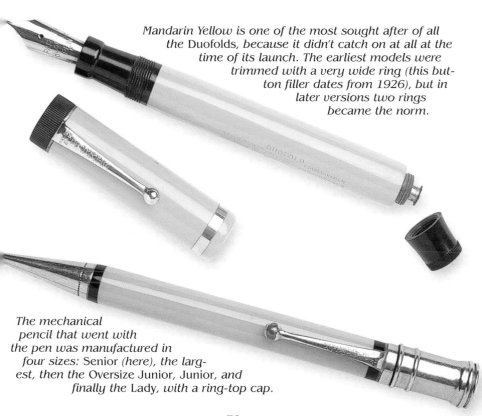

Mandarin Yellow is one of the most sought after of all the Duofolds, because it didn't catch on at all at the time of its launch. The earliest models were trimmed with a very wide ring (this button filler dates from 1926), but in later versions two rings became the norm.

The mechanical pencil that went with the pen was manufactured in four sizes: Senior (here), the largest, then the Oversize Junior, Junior, and finally the Lady, with a ring-top cap.

As Duofolds exist in a multitude of colors and sizes, this model can form the basis of a collection on its own. From ladies' models, as below, through vest-pocket pens with matching pencils, to office versions with pen holder and desk-set, including...

a clock and lamp! In the 1930s, Parker even went as far as to have matching penknives made to go with their new generation Duofolds, the word Streamlined *now being added to the name, as with the model below. There are also more recent reissues, such as the* Duofold Mandarin *(see page 190).*

Wahl Eversharp, with Parker, Waterman, and Sheaffer, is one of the "big four" names in pen making. But, unlike the others, the origin of the brand name was not an inventor but the merger of a number of pre-existing firms: the Wahl Adding Machine Company, Ever Sharp, a pencil manufacturer from Japan, and the Boston Fountain Pen Company. The first pen was launched in 1918: the Tempoint.

The pen on the opposite page comes from around 1920 and is in hard rubber, a material with which Wahl Eversharp kept faith—for rather too long in fact—following its purchase of the Washington Rubber Company in 1922. The pen on this page is in Radite, the name the firm used for celluloid. It is a forerunner of the Personal Point that was brought out in 1929.

Dating from 1923–24, this Conklin in black herringbone ebonite is the firm's first lever filler. At the time, Conklin was still making many crescent pen models (see page 49).

Another Conklin lever filler, in prettily colored celluloid known as Navy Blue and Cream (in fact it's more black than blue). It is dated 1926 and seems to be a precursor of the same company's Endura illustrated on pages 88 and 89.

A Sheaffer 3.25 made in 1924 or 1925. The reference number inscribed on the nib indicates the pen's selling price in dollars. Hence, quite distinct models can possess the same number in addition to their name. There are, for instance, Balance 3.25s.

Crescent fillers were manufactured by Conklin between 1901 and 1928, the two hard rubber models illustrated being from the end of its reign. When launched, the crescent filler carried all before it. A number of precious variants exist: red hard rubber, black and red marble, silver-filled filigree, and more or less elaborate gold- or silver-plated overlay. Two Italian makers have recently began distributing lines that employ the crescent system (see pages 206 and 207).

*Introduced at
the end of 1924, the
Endura continued in
production until 1932.
Conklin sold them with a com-
prehensive, totally unconditional
warranty. Following on where ebonite
left off, celluloid, such as in this sapphire
blue version, made its appearance in 1926.
The black and gold model on the facing page
was brought out in 1929.*

Many collectors are solely interested in fountain pens, purchasing just the pen and leaving the pencil in the lurch. But, to separate an original pen and pencil set is like buying one of two matching lamps or splitting up two volumes of a novel. If it's for financial reasons, well, you might be forgiven, but otherwise... It can't be for lack of room—pens are among the least space-hungry objects one could hope to collect!

After the Endura (shown here is a black and pearl version), which sold very well, another brilliant innovation arose, the Nozac (see page 108). In 1938 Conklin was sold off to new shareholders. The firm produced a few more lines, such as the Park-O-Type, the Waltham, and the Winchester, but these are considered far inferior in quality to those on which the company's reputation had been built. Conklin shut up shop permanently in 1947.

This black and pearl celluloid coloring is probably one of the most widespread. Every producer tried their hand at it, including Waterman for such prestige lines as its mythical Patrician. Shown here is a model made by Chilton from the end of the 1920s.

*From Wahl
Eversharp's* Personal
Point *line, this is a* Deco
Band, *from 1929. It differs from its direct predeces-
sor, the basic* Personal Point *model, by the Greek key
ornament around its cap band. Note too that, as with
almost every other pen made by the company, the clip is of
the rollerball type, enabling the pen to be slipped snugly into
the pocket without fear of damaging the fabric.*

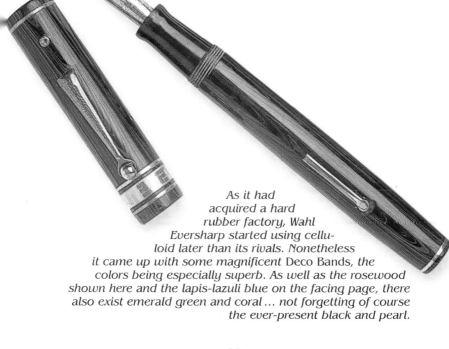

*As it had
acquired a hard
rubber factory, Wahl
Eversharp started using celluloid later than its rivals. Nonetheless
it came up with some magnificent Deco Bands, the
colors being especially superb. As well as the rosewood
shown here and the lapis-lazuli blue on the facing page, there
also exist emerald green and coral ... not forgetting of course
the ever-present black and pearl.*

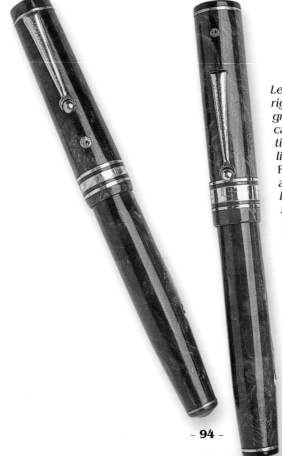

Left: an Equipoised and, right, a Deco Band, *both in green and bronze. Both carry the Gold Seal indicating they are guaranteed for life. They are part of the* Personal Point *range that allowed the nib ("point") to be changed in a matter of seconds. Advertising at the time boasted that this meant the pen could be rapidly adapted to the user's personal require-ments.*

Pelikan is a long-established concern making paints, pigments, carbon paper, and typewriter ribbons. Its first pen dates from 1925, however, about a century after its foundation. But coming late on the scene is not necessarily a curse in this market and, in 1929, with this 100 model, Pelikan developed a twist filling system that is still in use and is familiar notably to users of Montblanc pens.

Having spent much time and energy on hard rubber lines (as the Ripples on pages 71 to 75 show), Waterman finally threw its lot in with celluloid, launching the Patrician in 1929. It should be remembered though that ebonite held its own in some early versions of the Patrician, as with these two black pens whose fittings are of solid gold.

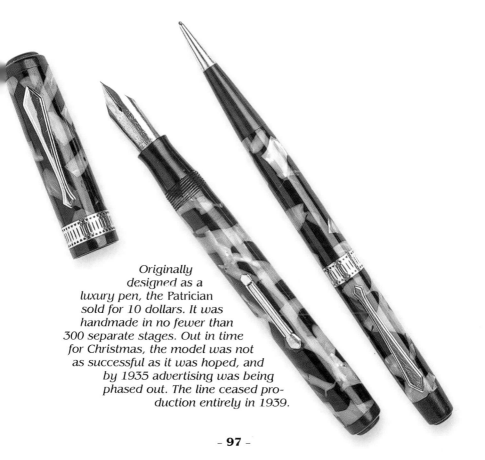

Originally designed as a luxury pen, the Patrician sold for 10 dollars. It was handmade in no fewer than 300 separate stages. Out in time for Christmas, the model was not as successful as it was hoped, and by 1935 advertising was being phased out. The line ceased production entirely in 1939.

In retrospect,
the Patrician can
be considered one of the finest
pieces ever to be manufactured by
Waterman. It is a cult model among collectors, and a pen-lover should be
acquainted with all its colors: Turquoise
(see page 281); Onyx (see page 219); Jet
(brilliant black); Emerald, a marbled green illustrated on page 96; and the black and pearl Nacre
(see page 97). In 1932, to these five original tones
was added this Moss Agate version in green marbled
with brown and gold.

Despite launching the Patrician in a blaze of publicity, proclaiming that it was the finest and most elegant fountain pen for men, "a triumph after almost half a century of Waterman successes," Waterman was soon marketing a Lady Patricia in 1930. This is a superb turquoise example.

*Sheaffer, in bring-
ing out the Balance
pen in 1930, made com-
peting models look passé.
Aviation was very much in the
air and aerodynamically "streamline"
forms were all the rage.*

And indeed the Balance is a very well balanced pen indeed. The model below is a Conklin Chicago, which, though close to Sheaffer's, came out fully ten years later. Note the striking colors of both these celluloids, the Conklin tint being known as "roseglow."

*From
1931 on,*
Balances *were
fitted with a new
reversible nib known as feather-
touch. Used in the normal fashion, it
offered extraordinary flexibility; turned
over, however, it was sufficiently stiff for
carbon copies. To allow for this the nib
was coated in palladium (the white tip section visible on the illustration).*

The firm of Sheaffer had already introduced a notable innovation with its warranties for the Lifetime line (see page 77). From 1924, the models it covered were marked with the White Dot. From 1935, the ball on the clip was re-designed flat, as on the black and pearl Balance shown here.

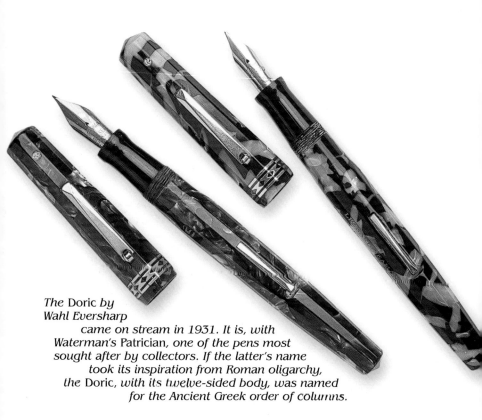

The Doric by
Wahl Eversharp
came on stream in 1931. It is, with
Waterman's Patrician, one of the pens most
sought after by collectors. If the latter's name
took its inspiration from Roman oligarchy,
the Doric, with its twelve-sided body, was named
for the Ancient Greek order of columns.

The Doric remained in the maker's catalog until 1941. It was marketed in fine colors with some exotic names: Kashmir Green, that on the facing page; Morocco, with a case of a rich red; Burma, a smoky gray nacre; Jet, a version in shiny black ebonite; the turquoise Cathay. Not many black and pearl versions (illustrated) were manufactured and only a few surviving pens are known worldwide.

If the Doric
was not as
triumphant as it
might have been, Extra by
Omas, which took up its lines, is a paragon
of longevity, having been made over a period
of sixty years. Depending on the year of production, the details of an Extra can vary widely. During
the War, for example, as metal was hard to come by,
caps were dressed with just three thin white rings
rather than with Greek fretwork. After hostilities ceased,
the superb frieze was restored to its rightful place.

*Launched in 1930 and produced for
a space of ten years, Itala, also by
the Italian firm of Omas, is fitted with
two nibs activated by a button at the
other end. The mechanics of this piston
filler are rather complicated, the advantage
being that one can write with two different
colored inks. On pages 318 and 319 appear two
other pens for writing with two inks.*

In 1932, Conklin also came up with
pen with faceted sides, the Nozac.
The barrel in some models
incorporates a transparent
word gauge indicating in
thousands the number
of words that could be
written with the ink
remaining in the cham-
ber! As the publicity material at the time proclaimed: "A
car without a gas gauge is like
a pen without a word
gauge."

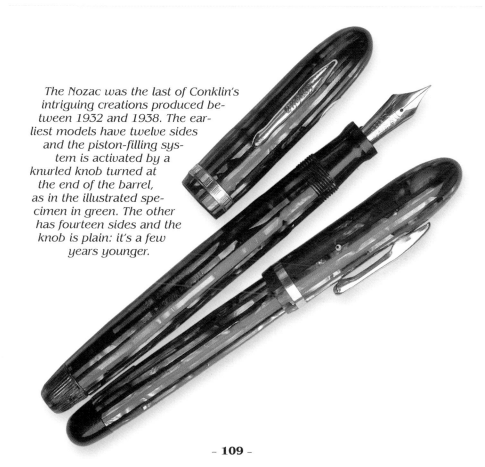

The Nozac was the last of Conklin's intriguing creations produced between 1932 and 1938. The earliest models have twelve sides and the piston-filling system is activated by a knurled knob turned at the end of the barrel, as in the illustrated specimen in green. The other has fourteen sides and the knob is plain: it's a few years younger.

*In March 1933, Parker made a great stir with the
Vacuum Filler, a name that reflected a new
type of filling system. The nib could be used
on both sides (one flexible, the other mani-
fold) and it was fitted with a new clip by
designer Joseph Platt. In the shape of
an arrow, it was to become Parker's
trademark. In this model the
nib too is marked with the
symbol.*

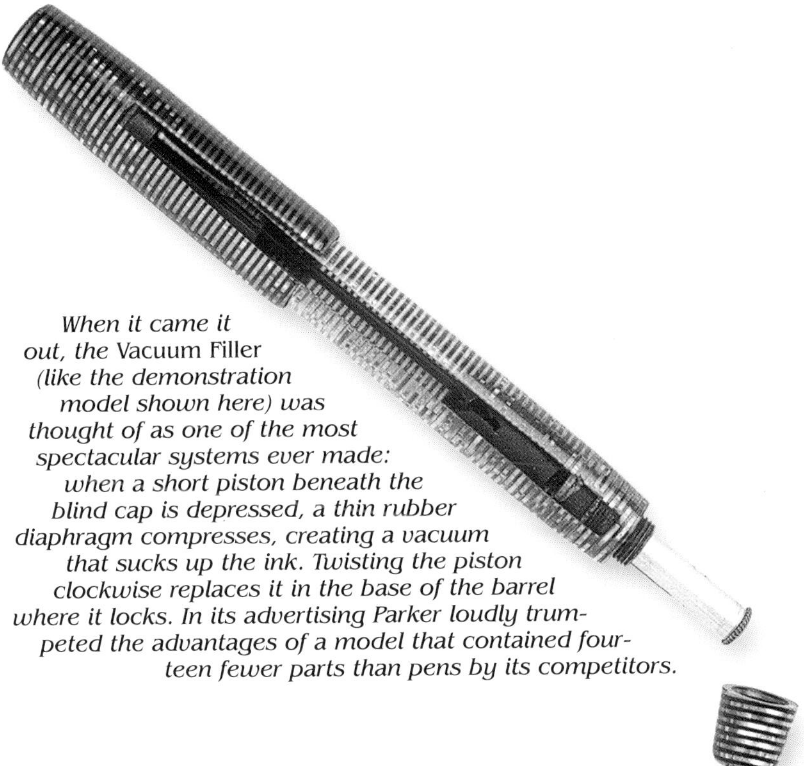

When it came it
out, the Vacuum Filler
(like the demonstration
model shown here) was
thought of as one of the most
spectacular systems ever made:
when a short piston beneath the
blind cap is depressed, a thin rubber
diaphragm compresses, creating a vacuum
that sucks up the ink. Twisting the piston
clockwise replaces it in the base of the barrel
where it locks. In its advertising Parker loudly trum-
peted the advantages of a model that contained fourteen fewer parts than pens by its competitors.

With its
overtones of
a vacuum cleaner, the
name "Vacuum Filler" was
soon replaced by the more
marketable "Vacumatic." Under this
mark, the brand sold like hot cakes,
especially those lines whose alternately
striped dark and light celluloid body allows
the ink level to be checked when the pen is
held up to a light source.

Kenneth Parker,
who had succeeded his
father at the firm, thought up the
idea of the Vacumatic. The story goes that its
color scheme was inspired by the New York skyline at
night. What is certain is that, until the 1940s, countless variations
on the line were issued, among them ones that transform into a
desk set as shown above. Over time, however, the system turned
out to be very fragile, and it is a rare thing indeed to find a fully
operational example.

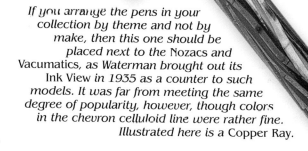

If you arrange the pens in your
collection by theme and not by
make, then this one should be
placed next to the Nozacs and
Vacumatics, as Waterman brought out its
Ink View in 1935 as a counter to such
models. It was far from meeting the same
degree of popularity, however, though colors
in the chevron celluloid line were rather fine.
Illustrated here is a Copper Ray.

In spite of its arrow-shaped cap clip and a celluloid case reminiscent of a Vacumatic, this pen is no Parker: it's an Extra Lucens by Omas, whose first models came off the production line in 1936, the present one dating from 1938. Its exemplary transparency is proof of this first-rate Italian maker's technical prowess.

*Just when the
American concern of Waterman
was entering stormy waters, the
company representing its interests in
France, Jif Waterman, popped up with a
novel adaptation of the glass cartridge
(Eagle had already had a similar idea some
fifty years earlier, see page 44). A real Innovation in 1936, the system was much feted by
aficionados—but by no one else. Perhaps it was a
tad ahead of its time...*

At the beginning
of the twentieth century, Waterman
set its sights on setting up a worth
while distribution network in Europe.
In 1914 Jules-Isidore Fagard became its
representative in France, going on in
1926 to create the company of Jif
Waterman, which took over the American
firm at a later juncture. In 1936, however,
when this other glass-cartridge model came out,
that wasn't yet on the table!

*Whereas the major
players were engaged in
Titanic struggles for market
share, smaller suppliers were
also employed in making interesting models. Le Bœuf is one such
company, whose name sounds French
but which actually worked out of
Springfield, Massachusetts.*

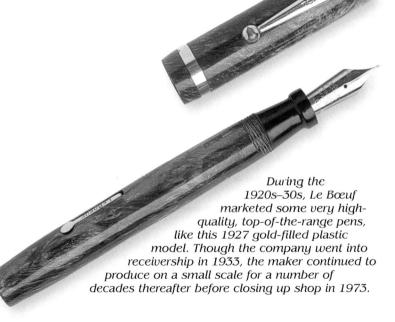

During the 1920s–30s, Le Bœuf marketed some very high-quality, top-of-the-range pens, like this 1927 gold-filled plastic model. Though the company went into receivership in 1933, the maker continued to produce on a small scale for a number of decades thereafter before closing up shop in 1973.

Names wise, here it's the opposite: Oldwin looks English enough but is in fact a French company to the core. It was founded in 1930 by Bruno Mora, father of André Mora whose reputation and store on rue Tournon, Paris, are well-known to collectors the world over. Oldwin originally set up shop on rue Charlot in the very heart of Paris.

These models are all
from the 1930s. The
one on the far right is not
made of celluloid but
Rhodoid, a material composed
of sheets of acetate cellulose. Note
the fine snake-head clip on the pen on
the facing page. André Mora has decided
to relaunch the Oldwin mark, and debut
pens should be out soon.

When it started, the Paris firm of Edac, which was to become Edacoto in 1920, was primarily a mechanical pencil manufacturer. In 1931, from around when this pen dates, it joined forces with the Italian Aurora company that went on to make a proportion of its fountain pens: the 200 Luxe shown here was a signally popular line.

Another Edacoto model from the 1930s. The advertising of the time presented the firm's product as "the pen for France." Edacoto ceased trading in 1950 following a last desperate bid with the cartridge pen. Like so many others, this company failed to hold its own against the rising ball-point tide.

The consummate artist Fernand Laureau won a Silver Medal at the International Exhibition of Decorative Arts in 1925. His superb niello silver models (see page 310) like this one are much in vogue with collectors, but the name of their designer is all but forgotten. It should be said in defense that, since he often subcontracted to major companies such as Parker, a large part of Fernand Laurcau's production is not marked as his.

To be a fountain pen collector also means showing an interest in this type of model. A no-name pen of the 1930s made in France. Nothing could be simpler. The nib is of a crude white metal—but for all that, the pen functions perfectly!

This beautifully
colored celluloid pen
from the 1930s was
made by Monogram Pen.
Like dozens of other smaller
concerns, such as Perry Pen,
Sanford & Bennett, or Wellcome
Pen, this company did not weather
the Great Crash that shook the economies
of the Western world in 1929.

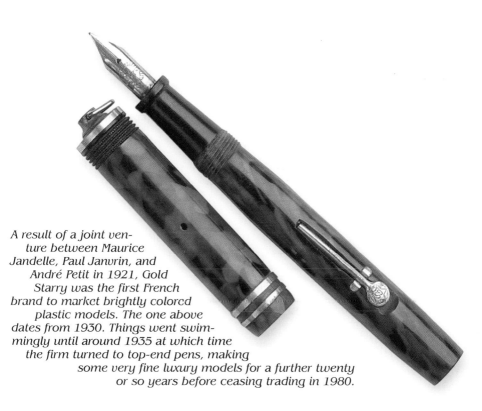

A result of a joint venture between Maurice Jandelle, Paul Janvrin, and André Petit in 1921, Gold Starry was the first French brand to market brightly colored plastic models. The one above dates from 1930. Things went swimmingly until around 1935 at which time the firm turned to top-end pens, making some very fine luxury models for a further twenty or so years before ceasing trading in 1980.

Set up in Boston in 1857, the Carter Ink Co. soon became one of the foremost ink producers in the United States. Between 1926 and 1931 it was also involved in fountain pen manufacture, having, it appears, bought out patents and purchased stock from Laughlin Pens (see page 345). The firm is best known for its quality lines, often in unusual colors. After the economic slump of 1929, Carter essentially concerned itself once again with ink production.

Around
1902 in
Boston, Seth Crocker
created the Crocker Pen. His
son Seth Chilton Crocker took over
the firm's reins, then, in 1923, came
up with the Chilton Pen, selling off the
Crocker Pen Co. in 1931. This model is a
1930s Chilton piston. See also page 341 for a
"holy water" model by the same company.

At first glance, this 1930s Swell could be mistaken for a Parker Duofold! It has the same overall size and a similar nib. More or less deliberate copy cats are legion in the world of pens and represent a good theme with which to start a collection—not least because such models often turn out to be much less costly than the authentic stars.

This 1930s Pilot, as well as presenting a very clear visible-ink section, possesses a capillary filling system, revolutionary for the time. No lever, no button, no rubber sac—just a rigid reservoir containing a spongy material. A very similar system would be employed by Parker in its famous 61 line fully thirty years later.

Étienne Forbin was initially a trading agent for a small American company. In 1912 he registered several brand names, among them Bayard and Excelsior. Some of his products were made at Arbois in the French Jura region. He was succeeded by his nephews some ten years later, and they changed the name of the company to Panici Frères et Cie, though the trademarks stayed the same. Nibs on Bayard models are engraved with the initials P. and F.

In the 1930s and for the three following decades, Bayard was a major player in the French marketplace. As there lived a medieval knight of the same name, Bayard's advertisements naturally made the most of the opportunity to allude to its products as being "fearless," "irreproachable," and so forth. The model on the facing page is a dazzling coral celluloid from about 1930; the piece below is marginally more recent.

Since there is no reason to ignore potential customers, in 1936 Wahl Eversharp launched the easy-on-the-pocket Wahl Oxford line. Available in a number of colors, these models too naturally enjoyed a lifetime guarantee, as signified by a white dot.

With very much the same idea in mind, Sheaffer also released a range of pens at that time using the brand name W.A.S.P., standing for W. A. Sheaffer Pens. In conjunction with these, the company also offered another low-cost line, the Craig.

Set up in Paris in 1919, the Unic brand dubbed its products, "the perfect pen," or else, "the pen that works"! It is true that its pens were of high quality, the finishes being especially remarkable. Among a wide range of models one finds fine black and red marble ebonite pens with filgree-type cases, but with a geometrical pattern. The one shown here came out in 1936.

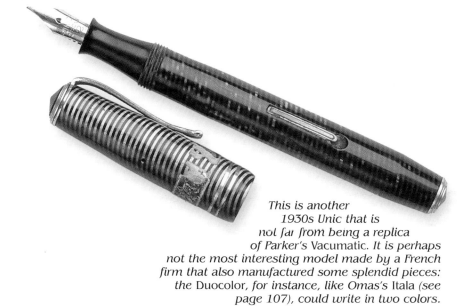

*This is another
1930s Unic that is
not far from being a replica
of Parker's Vacumatic. It is perhaps
not the most interesting model made by a French
firm that also manufactured some splendid pieces:
the Duocolor, for instance, like Omas's Itala (see
page 107), could write in two colors.*

Designed
in 1933 by the
German firm
Osmia, this pen seems
to anticipate some of the
future Montblancs. Founded in
1919, Osmia was bought up by
Parker in 1928 and then by Faber-
Castell. It is a pity that neither company
seems to have realized the potential of fine
models such as this one...

When this
Montblanc was
first put on the market
at the end of the 1930s, it
already incorporated many of
the features that were subsequently to lead to the success of the
flagship Meisterstück 149: the definitive
name of the brand, registered in 1911; the
white star on the cap that had already
appeared in 1913; the Meisterstück "line" from
1924; and a piston-filling system adopted in 1935.

The Premier was launched at the end of the 1930s and continued in production until 1945. It should be noted that the different names Sheaffer gave to its models correspond generally to the position occupied by a particular type in its line: hence the Premier and the Statesman designate top-quality large pens, the Sovereign corresponds to a standard model, while Excellence and Autograph refer to gold trim, etc.

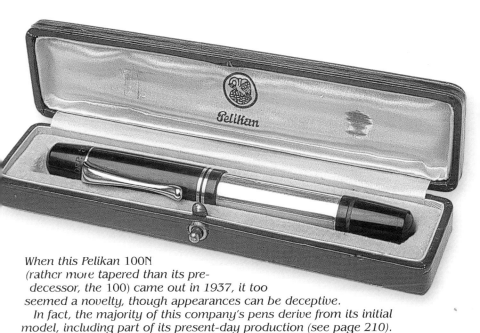

When this Pelikan 100N
(rather more tapered than its pre-
decessor, the 100) came out in 1937, it too
seemed a novelty, though appearances can be deceptive.
In fact, the majority of this company's pens derive from its initial
model, including part of its present-day production (see page 210).
The one shown above is made of gold, the original presentation
box considerably enhancing the interest of the piece.

This pen is the low-cost and slightly later version of Waterman's Hundred Year illustrated on the facing page. The earlier models were smaller and had a ribbed body and cap. The clip on this model is in the military style. US Army regulations stated that shirt pockets had to be buttoned down: as clips would look odd extending below the flap, they were placed very high on the pen.

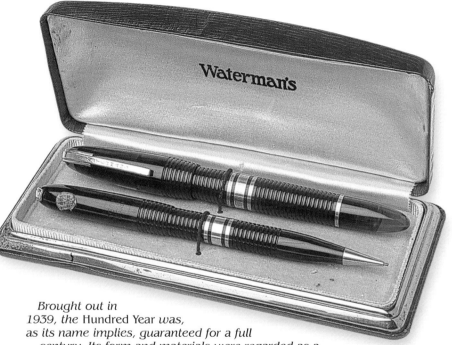

Brought out in
1939, the Hundred Year was,
as its name implies, guaranteed for a full
century. Its form and materials were regarded as a
real innovation for Waterman, as was its color range,
in transparent red, green, blue and black. Early versions were
trimmed with a triple band over a ribbed body. The bands was
later transferred to the cap. Waterman was also to manufacture
smooth-barrel versions.

After the fai-
lure of the Doric,
in 1940 Wahl Eversharp
underwent restructuring, abbreviating its
name to Eversharp. The earliest Skylines came
off the production line in the same year and met
with extraordinary success. This model was, however, the last hurrah for a company that in former times
had manufactured some marvelous pieces.

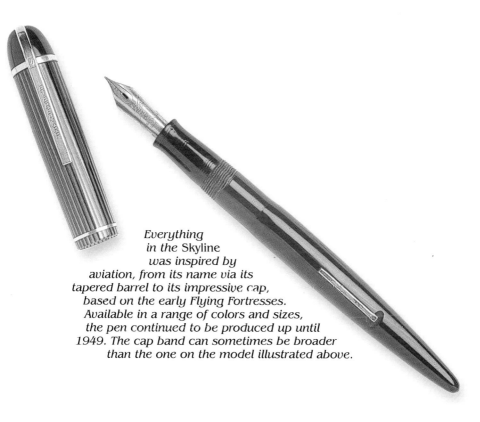

*Everything
in the* Skyline
*was inspired by
aviation, from its name via its
tapered barrel to its impressive cap,
based on the early Flying Fortresses.
Available in a range of colors and sizes,
the pen continued to be produced until
1949. The cap band can sometimes be broader
than the one on the model illustrated above.*

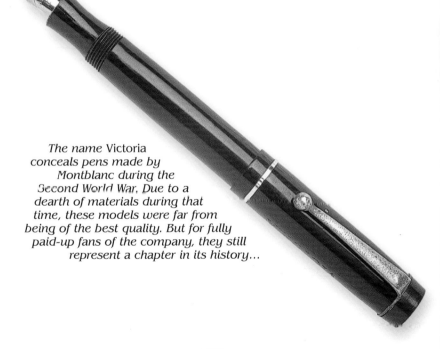

The name Victoria
conceals pens made by
Montblanc during the
Second World War. Due to a
dearth of materials during that
time, these models were far from
being of the best quality. But for fully
paid-up fans of the company, they still
represent a chapter in its history...

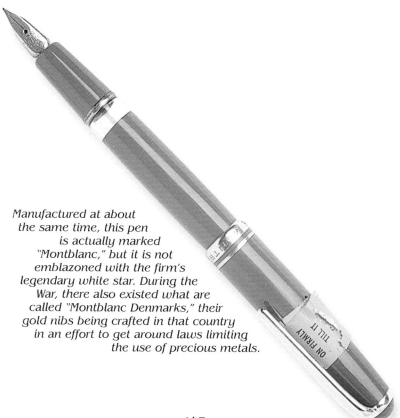

Manufactured at about
the same time, this pen
is actually marked
"Montblanc," but it is not
emblazoned with the firm's
legendary white star. During the
War, there also existed what are
called "Montblanc Denmarks," their
gold nibs being crafted in that country
in an effort to get around laws limiting
the use of precious metals.

II

MODERN
fountain pens

Any fountain pen that was manufactured after the Second World War can be considered "modern." They are modern in respect of their technical specifications, their filling systems, their color range, their materials—in short, they exhibit "modernity" when compared to their pre-war predecessors. Among them a number of avant-garde models were heavily influenced by aeronautics—at least until the interstellar world and the rocket refined styles still further. More recently, an extravagant "back to the future" has taken place: the turn of the millennium sees the height of modernity in an oft-repeated return to the classic lines of the 1930s and 1940s, to the aesthetic of a time on which, whatever may be thought of it, present-day society is based.

Launched to celebrate the 51st birthday of Parker's foundation in 1888, the Parker 51 marks a turning-point in the history of the modern fountain pen. Tested out first in Brazil in 1939–40, where it was not—it must be admitted—welcomed with open arms, it was nonetheless thrust on the American market in 1941. The Parker 51 quickly became a symbol of modernity: the line endured for 37 years and sold 50 million!

The Parker 51
owes its characteristic
hooded tubular nib to László
Moholy-Nagy, one of the staff at the celebrated Bauhaus school of applied art who were turfed out
of Germany by Hitler. Many of these artists made their way to
Chicago from where they exercised significant sway over
contemporary American design.

In addition to its ultra-modern looking, streamlined form, the Parker 51 owed its popularity to a new fast-drying ink, Quick Ink. Housed within the body of the pen, not only was the hooded nib well protected but it also prevented the ink from evaporating too quickly.

With its vast range of colors and lines that have changed over time, the Parker 51 forms a good basis for a collection in itself (see also page 148). On this photograph, the brown model is one of the earliest. The little blue diamond on the clip indicates that it benefited from a twenty-five year guarantee.

This pen intended for the American Legion was assembled in 1942 by Morrison. The insignia on the top of the cap is made of copper and enamel. At the same period, Morrison also produced a red celluloid pen of a similar type with United States and British flags.

*A desk-top version of the Parker 51 dating from 1945.
The center piece with the trumpet is held to the base
by a magnet that over time has lost none of its
strength: even using both hands, it's almost
impossible to yank it off!*

FOR YOU WHO CHERISH FINE THINGS—YOUR...

MOORE *finger tip* **PEN**

AND MATCHING PENCIL

Moore's Fingertip
began production in 1946.
It was supposed to challenge the
supremacy of the Parker 51. In fact the
nib is pretty good and really did seem to
come from another world, as advertising put it at
the time. A Fingertip is a must in any 1940s-centered collection, but today it is difficult to come by.

Connoisseurs are of the opinion that the Fingertip failed to attract its anticipated market share simply because it still looked too much like models of the 1930s. After this setback, Moore went on to create the Specialist, before closing down in 1956.

The first Stylomine 303s
were produced in 1930. The
pump-filling system was,
however, very close to Parker's
earlier Vacumatic, and functioned
by unscrewing the blind cap and
depressing a small rubber sac several
times. This model dates from the 1950s, by
which time a new accordion-shape sac was
employed that increased the capacity of
the ink reservoir still further.

Simple but effective and very contemporary in appearance, this pen is a 1950s Edacoto. In its advertising, the brand boasted that its nibs were crafted in its own workshops and hand-finished, giving them superb "attack."

Nothing could be more
classical than this
Montegrappa from the
1950s. This Italian concern,
which set up in business in 1912,
devoted its energies to creating the
most exuberant styles.

Once it turned to Western markets, Namiki needed to adopt a more "international" sounding name. It chose Pilot, which was easy to pronounce in every language, not least by the GIs occupying Japan in the 1950s, when the above pen was released. Nowadays, depending on the market, Pilot or Namiki pens can be found.

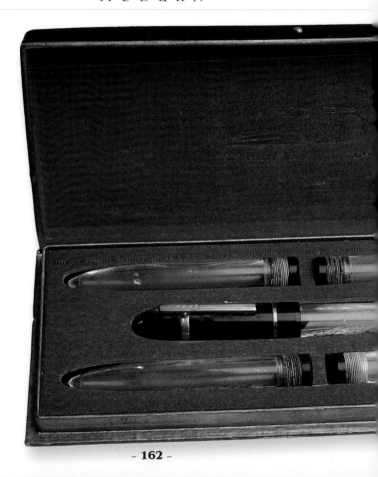

The name Tank 400 is a homage to the wea-
pons of the Second World War, which had ended
shortly before this pen saw the light of day. It is
an original 1947 model, the cartridge being integral with the body. To refill it, one had simply to
screw into the nib unit one of the four fresh
Plexiglas "cartridges" supplied with the case.
The originators of this concept, the firm of
Pierre Baignol, boldly declared that, with a
Tank 400, "no obstacle can stand in your
way"! Except that the idea never actually got
off the ground.

In the 1940s,
Rally launched a
pen with which, it
punningly proclaimed,
"everyone can rally
round." Though the brand
name is English to the ear—this was de rigueur at
the time—the models were actually crafted in the
heart of Paris's twentieth arrondissement.

In 1921, the firm born in 1916 under the name Manufacture Parisienne de Porte-Plume Réservoir became La Plume d'Or ("gold pen"), the Météore here being one of its best-known brand identities. This model dates from the 1950s. In keeping with its trading name, La Plume d'Or was also the largest European supplier of gold nibs, but the business folded in 1956.

Between 1952 and 1959, Sheaffer's Saratoga was produced in any number of colors, including pastel pink and blue. It was fitted with the intriguing Snorkel filling system, described on page 316.

At the same time, Sheaffer also offered pens such as this Sentinel Deluxe, which, like the Saratoga, is equipped with the Snorkel filling system. This model is fitted with a tubular nib, however. Of the same size and with the same system, the Sovereign employed a classic nib design.

Set up in Bonn in 1875, Soennecken was one of the largest German manufacturers, not only of pens but also of steel nibs. Its factories were laid waste in the Second World War and the business found it difficult to get back on track. In the 1950s, from when this pen dates, Soennecken collaborated for a time with the French brand Bayard, before ceasing trade entirely in 1967.

Though the English company De La Rue had existed for over a hundred years, it was 1905 before its Onoto pens made an appearance (see also page 43). This model of the "K" line, from 1955, is a riposte to Parker's 51, but its launch did not prevent the august London operation from shutting its doors three years later.

Conway and Stewart are not, as might be expected, the names of the two founders of the business, but of an acting duo who were top of the bill when the company was set up in 1902! The decorated "cracked ice" case of the 58, launched in 1950, is a favorite among collectors. It was available in both black and blue.

*Feeling
the aftershocks
of the 1950s invention of
the ball-point pen more than
most, Conway and Stewart put their faith in originality with the Floral pen. In spite of its obvious charm,
the model was a fiasco from which the British company never recovered. Specialists maintain that only a
few hundred of these pens, launched in 1955, were
ever produced. The firm has recently been revived
and it now offers, among other models, a reissue of
the Floral pen, not in celluloid but in lacquer. Its
prices are unfortunately exorbitant...*

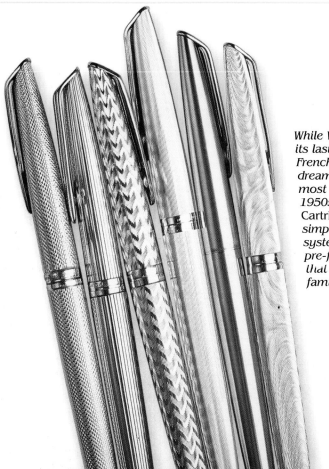

While Waterman was on its last legs in the US, its French arm, Jif Waterman, dreamed up one of the most novel ideas of the 1950s: the CF, or Cartridge Filler. Quite simply, it was the filling system using plastic pre-filled ink cartridges that has since become familiar to us all.

Produced from 1954, the Cartridge Filler was so successful that it allowed Jif Waterman to keep afloat in spite of its serious difficulties. In 1969, Jules Fagard's granddaughter Francine Gomez took over the reins of the company whose name became Waterman S.A. in 1971. In a matter of months she had bought up what remained of the American arm that had ceased trading in 1958 and took over trademarks in Canada, England, and Asia. In 1987 the firm returned, as it were, to its birthplace, being taken over by an American giant, the Gillette group. Its models now appeared cheek by jowl with those of its long-standing competitor Parker!

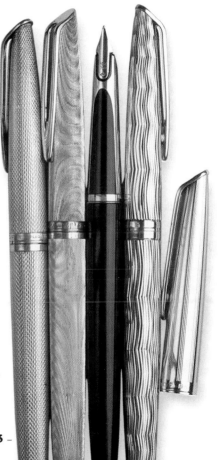

As the photos over the preceding double-page
spread show, the CF was assembled with
many different cases: gold-filled, gold-
plated or with gold-colored metal finish,
silver, silver-plated, or steel, with
striped, barleycorn, chevron, or
brushed patterns, etc. These
illustrated here are lacquer
and date from 1970.

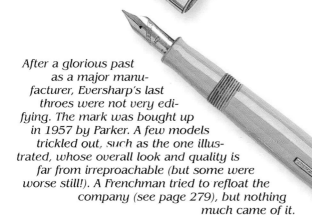

After a glorious past as a major manufacturer, Eversharp's last throes were not very edifying. The mark was bought up in 1957 by Parker. A few models trickled out, such as the one illustrated, whose overall look and quality is far from irreproachable (but some were worse still!). A Frenchman tried to refloat the company (see page 279), but nothing much came of it.

In the mid-1950s a pinnacle of perfection was attained by Montblanc in a piece with the well-deserved name of Meisterstück *(or* Masterpiece*). This* 149 *piston filler is the largest in size: it differs from the* 147 *which is fitted for cartridges to make it more practical for the traveler.*

Those of gloomy disposition may lament the fact that the Masterpiece has suffered from overexposure, being available in shopping malls, supermarkets, and duty-free stores the world over. But it is still an undeniable marvel of a fountain pen that can stay unused in a drawer for a year only to start up perfectly the moment the nib touches paper.

Banking on mirroring the success of the Parker 51, the firm launched the 61 on the market in 1956. This example dates from a year before the official launch of the model and is one of the few prototypes with the barrel open beneath the nib. It is through this aperture that the ink enters and rises up by capillary action into the reservoir containing a spongy material. The idea was dropped as the pen had constantly to be wiped clean of ink stains.

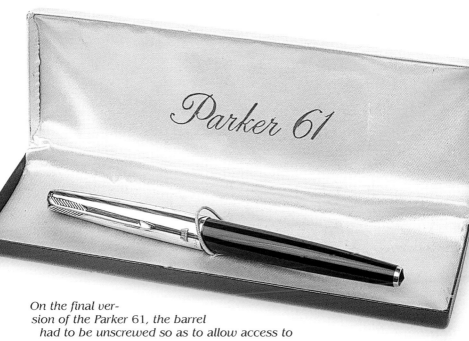

On the final ver-
sion of the Parker 61, the barrel
had to be unscrewed so as to allow access to
the spongy bladder within. This system, though simple in
theory, was not nearly so in practice and, above all, filling
was a protracted, bothersome affair.

In spite of its initially lukewarm reception, the Parker 61 became available in a host of finishes and continued in production up to the mid-1960s. Certain models incorporate a small arrow design protecting the nib (see page 243). The ones here are 61 MK2s.

This Sheaffer model is called the PFM—the "Pen for Men"! With its inlaid nib-unit looking unashamedly like a Cadillac wing, it chimed in well with the prevailing style when it came out in 1959.

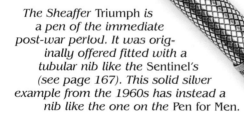

The Sheaffer Triumph *is
a pen of the immediate
post-war period. It was originally offered fitted with a
tubular nib like the Sentinel's
(see page 167). This solid silver
example from the 1960s has instead a
nib like the one on the* Pen for Men.

*This is perhaps one
of the most aerodynamic of all pens:
a Pilot Murex from 1971. In spite of its hyper-
modern lines, it in fact represents a kind of
"back to basics": the nib is an all-in-one integral
unit, exactly like the goose quill of old!*

It would be unjust to pass over the revolution represented by the appearance of the Visor Pen in the 1960s, and the slightly later Stypen. Thanks to good-quality steel nibs, fountain pens that had been the preserve of the adult market could now be aimed at children. Though colorful enough, early models were relatively understated. They subsequently lost all their inhibitions, becoming available in every imaginable decor. If you are thinking of starting up your own collection, you'll need to be patient: several hundred designs exist.

These superb silver-filled and silver-gilt Sheaffer pens are worthy of their name: Nostalgia. They are 1975 reissues of filigree pens formerly made by the Ford Madison company.

From the end of the 1980s, this 88 by Aurora is a less aerodynamic revamp of a 1947 model designed by Marcello Nizzoli. The original had a hooded nib of similar type to the Parker 51.

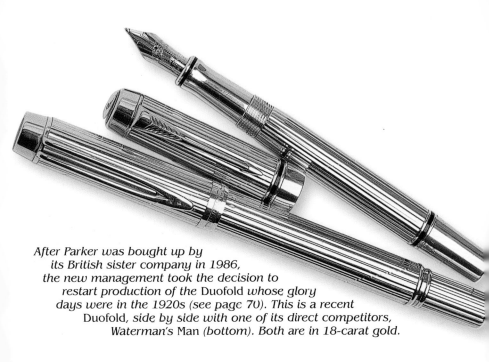

*After Parker was bought up by
its British sister company in 1986,
the new management took the decision to
restart production of the Duofold whose glory
days were in the 1920s (see page 70). This is a recent
Duofold, side by side with one of its direct competitors,
Waterman's Man (bottom). Both are in 18-carat gold.*

These three Duofolds *offer living proof that computers have not yet killed off handwriting. As long as pens as splendid as these remain on the market, there's hope for us all.*

In 1945, Dwight D. Eisenhower
ratified the German surrender
with a Duofold. *The favorite
pen of Colette, a writer
whose idiosyncrasy was
never in question, was a
Mandarin Yellow Duofold.
Wielding one of the 10,000 in
this relaunched style, you too
can dream of becoming
President or a great novelist!*

Although still a
young thing, the
Stipula brand, founded
in 1973 in Florence, has
come up with models that
seem to hark back to the
finest models of old, such as this
retractable nib Iris, whose colors
are reminiscent of the black and
pearls so popular in the 1930s.

This fine limited-series pen by Omas is more classic in shape than its companion on the facing page, and its originality lies in its color. Called Harlequin, it takes its name from the Italian commedia dell'arte *character.*

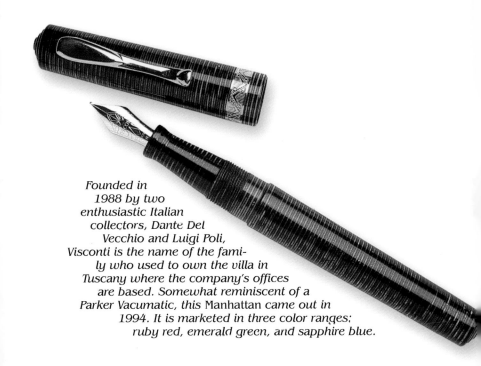

Founded in
1994 by two
enthusiastic Italian
collectors, Dante Del
Vecchio and Luigi Poli,
Visconti is the name of the family who used to own the villa in
Tuscany where the company's offices
are based. Somewhat reminiscent of a
Parker Vacumatic, this Manhattan came out in
1994. It is marketed in three color ranges:
ruby red, emerald green, and sapphire blue.

These Extra-Lucens are a "new-old" stock pen by Omas of a model originally launched in the 1930s (see page 115). Note the splendid coloring of the celluloid, a material that has not yet been quite ousted by today's resins and that high-end manufacturers have kept faith with, in spite of its being troublesome to work. In effect, celluloid production cannot be totally mechanized.

Founded in 1911, the Elmo company permanently adopted the name Montegrappa after the First World War as a tribute to the legendary Italian offensive on October 24, 1918, that witnessed the victory of the Italian army over German and Austrian forces.

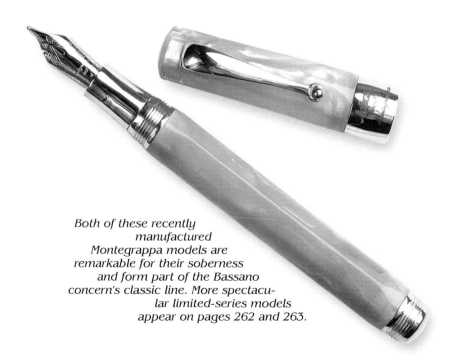

Both of these recently
manufactured
Montegrappa models are
remarkable for their soberness
and form part of the Bassano
concern's classic line. More spectacular limited-series models
appear on pages 262 and 263.

The three Cartier brothers, Louis-Joseph Jacques-Théodule, and Pierre-Camille, did much to enhance the company that their grandfather had set up in 1847 by promoting its name respectively in Paris, London and New York. In complement to its focus on jewelry and watches, Cartier turned to fountain pens in 1924

After some very contemporary designs in the 1970s, especially in its Ovale *and* Must *lines, Cartier turned back to more classical and elegant forms in the series named for the founder of the dynasty, Louis Cartier. Opposite is a resin model, and below a silver-plated version. They can be ordered directly from the jeweler in any combination of metals and precious stones.*

Rouge et Noir—*one of Montblanc's most famous early lines (see page 55) was reissued by the company in 2000. The one illustrated has a retractable nib and has the advantage of being a cartridge filler.*

One of the limited
edition series that
Montblanc has been pro-
ducing since 1992, this
Charlemagne is dated 2000.
The twist silver case over resin is
trimmed in gold-plate. See pages
288–291 for other models, especially
the series devoted to great writers.

Titanium is a highly resistant and lightweight material, which is used in aviation as well as in pen construction. This Omas T2 was launched in the year 2000. It has faceted sides, as do many pens in this Italian-based company's lines.

From the studio of Michel Audiard, Le Bambou is nicknamed "the head of state's pen," since one was presented to French President Jacques Chirac. That was a solid-silver model, the first in a series of twelve. The remaining eleven are no doubt awaiting other world leaders...

Waterman now has its head office in Newhaven, southern England, and its pens are produced in both England and France. At the present time, it is one of the most forward-looking names, offering models for all pockets, like these recently launched resin Carenes.

Waterman came up with the
Edson in 1993 and it is equally
available in blue and red. Its name
offers a tribute to the founder of the
business, Lewis Edson Waterman. Remarkable for an engaging symmetry between
nib-unit and cap, its barrel is in
styrene-acrylonitrile, a transparent material
that has, like the cap, been surface-treated with
ultraviolet rays. The pen represents an entente cor-
diale between modernist classicism and
advanced technology.

If there are any lingering doubts as to whether pen design is returning to its past for inspiration, these two pens will dispel them. They are both modern Italian lines that have co-opted the crescent-filler system developed by Conklin in 1897. The one on this page is by Stipula, while that opposite is a Visconti Copernicus, equipped with a traveling ink-well that enables the pen to be filled on the move. These two models marry the charm of systems that form part of the glorious history of fountain pen manufacture to the reliability of an up-to-date product.

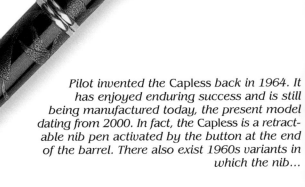

Pilot invented the Capless back in 1964. It has enjoyed enduring success and is still being manufactured today, the present model dating from 2000. In fact, the Capless is a retractable nib pen activated by the button at the end of the barrel. There also exist 1960s variants in which the nib...

... is retracted by turning a button. As it has survived on the market for a long time, the Capless has been produced in many different materials. The model on the facing page is exceptional, however, in being lacquered.

The Pelikan 400
first came out in
1951 and since then it
has never been out of production. The German compa-
ny's 1000 model, the largest in the
line, is of more recent conception.
Both are in the firm's hallmark colors of
green and black.
Since 1984, Pelikan has formed part of
a Swiss-based conglomerate.

The Toledo is a
makeover of a model
decorated with a pelican
design, the clip too being in
the shape of the bird's bill.
A niello technique is used for the
silver casework, which is then gilded
vermeil. There is also a limited series in
colored silver. The two-tone nib has been
delicately chased by hand.

The offices of Caran
d'Ache (whose name
means "pencil" in
Russian) have been located
in Geneva since 1924. It is a
company reputed for artists'
supplies, introducing
its first fountain pens in 1974,
with limited series intended for
the collector's market coming
on stream in 1995.

*Caran d'Ache's Leman model, in lacquer and silver-
plate, came out in 2001. In addition to its own
models, the company also makes pens for other lea-
ding names such as Bulgari and Tiffany's, as well as
special lines for Mercedes Benz and Rolls-Royce.*

From a family with its roots in England, Alonzo Townsend Cross was an inventor. As well as making the Stylographic Pen (see page 327), he collaborated in the development of a steam engine intended to power his pen-manufacturing workshop, but which he also adapted to a carriage, thereby producing the first motor vehicle in Providence, Rhode Island.

In 1996, on the occasion of the 150th anniversary of Cross's foundation, the firm relaunched this pen, one of its flagship products from the 1930s. pOn the facing page are two Townsends, one in sterling silver and the other gold-plated. They take their inspiration from an Art Deco model manufactured long ago by the company.

III

PRECIOUS
fountain pens

Depending on individual taste, any vintage pen can be precious in a collector's eyes. The only stipulation is that it should have attained a certain level of quality in its components and manufacture. It is fortunate that during the war years, when the world was suffering from a severe shortage of gold, a number of more enlightened connoisseurs were instrumental in saving countless models from being melted down. The fountain pen also went through hard times in the 1950s as the ball-point carried all before it. But everyone knows that what goes around comes around, and fountain pens are back in vogue once again. Manufacturers have thus found it imperative to bring out contemporary models that remain exclusive because they are made in limited quantities and often out of costly or rare materials.

A pen may be precious because of its state of preservation, above all when it is made out of a fragile material such as celluloid that flakes and fades after a time. From this point of view, these Patricians, a model considered one of the finest in the repertory, are faultless.

On its launch, Waterman offered the Patrician in five colors, among which the Turquoise, the brown and honey marble case of the facing page, and the Onyx beige-brown marble illustrated here. Others are to be seen on pages 96–99.

Even if they
don't look out
of this world, all
vintage pens are pre-
cious—especially when
they represent an event in
the history of the pen like the 1898 Parker
No. 1 here, which dates from before the estab-
lishment of the Parker Pen Company. It is in
marble hard rubber and is fitted with the famous
lucky curve system (see page 40).

Wirt was one of the
biggest twentieth-
century suppliers that for one
glorious fifteen-year period pro-
duced more pens than all of its competitors combined.
Kicking off in 1878 on a craft basis, Paul Wirt soon
converted to mechanized manufacture, designing the
machinery himself. This fine 1915 gold-plated taper-cap
model comes from the heyday of a firm that shut up
shop permanently at the end of the 1930s.

A number of pen fanciers reckon Waterman's Indian Scroll to be one of the classiest pens ever made. This specimen from 1905 is a magnificent piece with a solid-gold full-overlay case. Models made between 1910 and 1920 also come in silver-filled overlay and half-overlay, covering only a proportion of the pen.

The 34 was
the pen that
marked the official
birth of the W. A. Sheaffer
Pen Company in 1913. It is
fitted with a lever-filling system, the first of its kind, with a
side lever pressing down directly
on the rubber sac in the barrel of
the pen. This original model in a
remarkably fine state of preservation is
gold-filled. Sheaffer has recently launched
a replica version.

Two particularly fine pens of the 1910s by Mabie Todd & Co. This company, founded in New York in 1873, opened an outlet in London in 1884. It had a reputation for producing fountain pens of high quality, and the English branch swelled in size to the point of absorbing its American parent company. The whole was bought out by Biro Pens in 1952.

On the model on
the facing page,
the ink-feed is placed
on top of the nib. This
"overfeed" process was
soon jettisoned for aesthetic reasons since it spoiled the
pen's purity of line. The nib on
this rare silver pen is an "underfeed"—the piece has been photo-
graphed upside-down.

Parker's Snake pen is a
truly legendary model (see
facing page), but this curling
serpent is signed Waterman.
Older than its Parker counterpart, it
dates from 1910. Note the superb
long cap that, once placed on the end of
the barrel, makes the whole the spitting
image of an old-fashioned "penner."

*Probably
one of the most
sought-after fountain
pens of all time, the Parker Snake is
signed with an H for "Heath," a famous
New York jeweler. This model dates from
1916 and is one of the rare end-button
fillers, the line being most often an eye-
dropper. A modern version of the type
can be seen on page 283.*

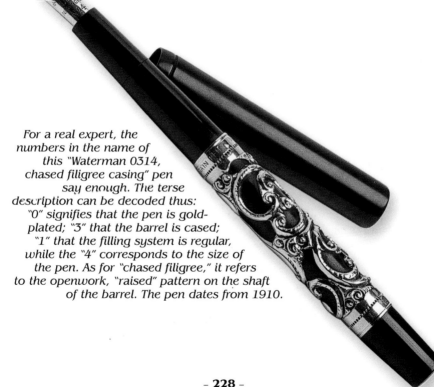

For a real expert, the numbers in the name of this "Waterman 0314, chased filigree casing" pen say enough. The terse description can be decoded thus: "0" signifies that the pen is gold-plated; "3" that the barrel is cased; "1" that the filling system is regular, while the "4" corresponds to the size of the pen. As for "chased filigree," it refers to the openwork, "raised" pattern on the shaft of the barrel. The pen dates from 1910.

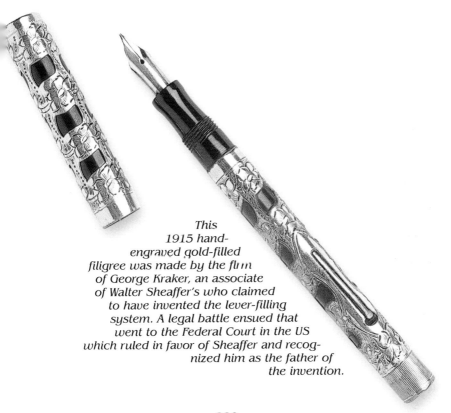

*This
1915 hand-
engraved gold-filled
filigree was made by the firm
of George Kraker, an associate
of Walter Sheaffer's who claimed
to have invented the lever-filling
system. A legal battle ensued that
went to the Federal Court in the US
which ruled in favor of Sheaffer and recog-
nized him as the father of
the invention.*

A Parker 41 filigree, from 1915. If Waterman's very practical numbering system had a precise meaning (see page 228), Parker's on the other hand conveyed nothing in particular. Not very helpful for fountain pen collectors...

These three filigrees offer proof if proof be needed that, even in the early days, once a particular type of pen became a hit with the buying public, other companies would soon be following suit. From top to bottom: a 1405 by Edward Todd; a 01.02 by John Holland (George Parker's first employee), and, finally, a Waterman 0514.

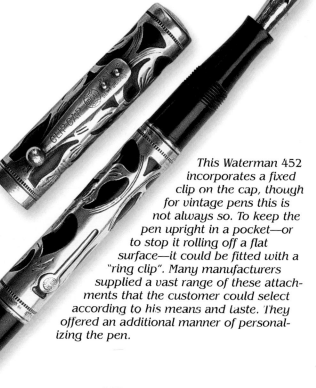

This Waterman 452 incorporates a fixed clip on the cap, though for vintage pens this is not always so. To keep the pen upright in a pocket—or to stop it rolling off a flat surface—it could be fitted with a "ring clip". Many manufacturers supplied a vast range of these attachments that the customer could select according to his means and taste. They offered an additional manner of personalizing the pen.

If gold filigree designs (or, as here, silver) are common enough on black hard rubber, they are much rarer on red, a color known as "cardinal." This is a 452 model by Waterman, an eye-dropper from 1910–12. Another pen of this type is illustrated on page 64.

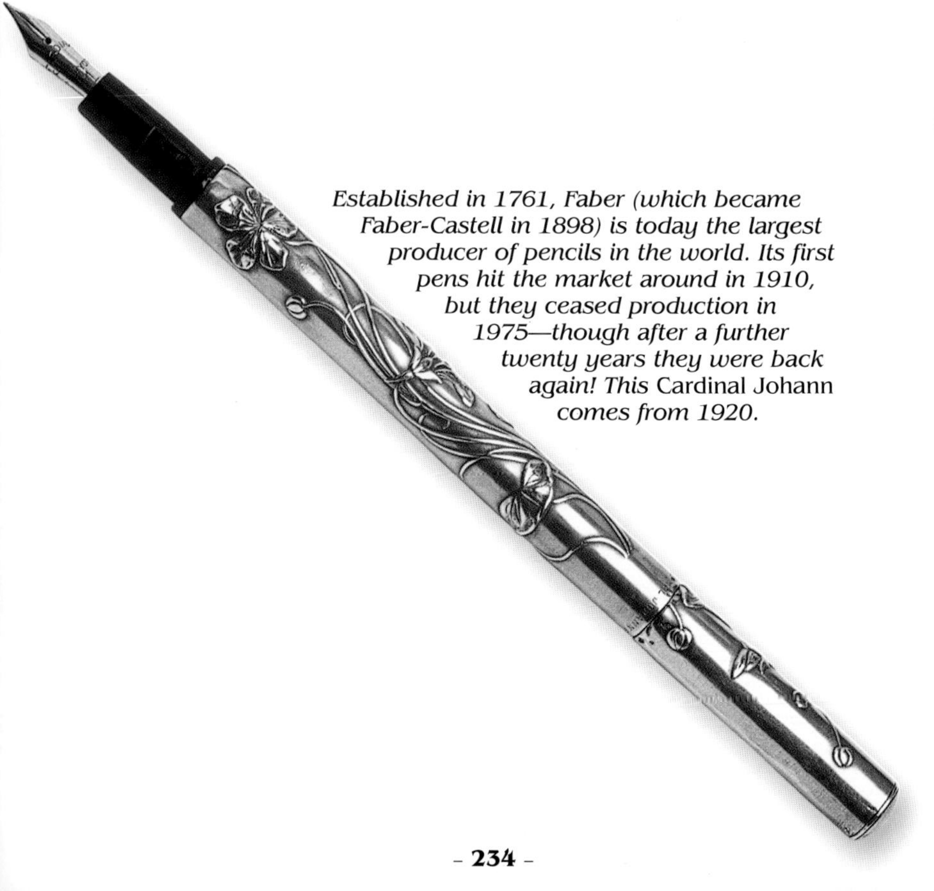

Established in 1761, Faber (which became Faber-Castell in 1898) is today the largest producer of pencils in the world. Its first pens hit the market around in 1910, but they ceased production in 1975—though after a further twenty years they were back again! This Cardinal Johann *comes from 1920.*

This pretty gold piece was made by the Carey Pen Co. The operation was founded in New York in 1890, but it proved to be short-lived, folding in 1915.

In America, the term "continental" is conventionally used to designate most of the overlays made in Europe, many of which were produced in Italy. This Waterman 42½ dates from 1925.

A superb "continental" case over an unusual red ebonite. This complete filling is known as "end covered"; when the casing stops before the end, the term is "low-end covered." Note the charming profile on the cap of this Waterman 42 from 1930.

Founded in 1918 by Ryosuke Namiki, the Pilot company is today a colossus of the writing instrument industry. It was Namiki who, around 1925, came up with the idea of lacquering pens using the traditional Japanese technique of maki-e. The reason was to forestall some of the problems with hard rubber which does not take color very well...

...and tarnishes over time. In the 1930s, the firm became associated with Dunhill and, trading under the name Dunhill-Namiki, conjured up a number of genuine master-pieces. On the facing page are two 1990 Namikis: left, Kachimushi ("dragonflies"), and right Rôkaku.
The model shown below is a vintage piece from the 1930s.

Another
Japanese lac-
quer fountain pen
decorated with a somewhat risqué scene.
In the 1920s, Pilot was the first company in
its own country to provide nibs flexible
enough to write Japanese characters in the correct way. There was then a pen revolution as
wide-ranging as anything that happened in the West
since in Japan it replaced the traditional brush!

Made by the jeweler Lefebvre, from the same family that today often works for Omas (see page 246), this tortoise-shell pen is remarkable for its understatement. The fragile material is rarely employed in pen manufacture. The model, from the 1930s, also possesses a fine gold clip.

Known universally as Big Red to collectors, Parker's red hard rubber Duofold is one of the most famous of all fountain pens. Another is illustrated on page 70, though it lacks a clip band, like the earliest examples. The pen shown here, dating from 1924, has only a single girdle. Versions with two bands are more recent still. A case of this kind, particularly of such a rich orange hue, and complete with mechanical pencil, is difficult to get hold of nowadays.

As noted earlier,
the Parker 61 did not
meet with the reception the
company hoped for (see pages
178–180). Nonetheless, there exist some
first-rate examples, such as the 18-carat
gold-filled specimen from 1960 shown
above. Note the arrow emblem on the tip of
the hood that serves to protect the nib.

This ebon-
ite number
called the
"Abraham Lincoln"
could equally well
have figured in the
chapter dedicated to un-
usual fountain pens: in an
amethyst in the top of the cap
is set a fragment of the epony-
mous President's DNA! In the same
vein—though without the DNA—
the American firm of Krone also
distributes a violet-toned
William Shakespeare. Truly spectacular!

*A Cartier
Bamboo in solid gold
dating from the 1920s. Launched in 1936, the models in real
bamboo wood (here, a mechanical pencil) were an immediate
hit—a success, it should be said, aided and abetted by
Marlene Dietrich and the Duchess of Windsor! Both types of
pens have been through numerous reincarnations.*

In a limited edition of 30, this 1992 pen was Omas's tribute to Christopher Columbus and portrays the main episodes in the discovery of America engraved by Gérard Lefebvre in thick gold-leaf. This model is called Almirante, signifying "Lord of the Sea" (the name being derived from the Arabic al-amir).

Created on the occasion of the 75th birthday of Ferrari, an Italian house based in Varese, this Etra model is made of ebony, a dense, hard wood that is particularly difficult to work. It is decorated entirely with tiny lengths of chain, handmade from a single thickness of wire, that are intertwined and then soldered. If some pens might be said not quite to deserve the description, "filigree" (see page 60), this piece certainly does!

In German Meisterstück means "masterpiece"— and how apt it is for a solid platinum version of Montblanc's cult pen, the 149! In addition to Montblanc's own gold-filled version, many jewelers have made cases for this model.

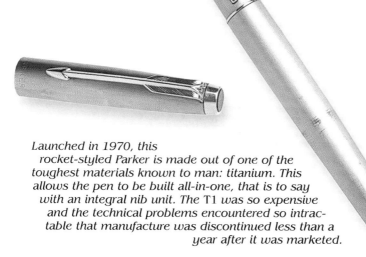

Launched in 1970, this
rocket-styled Parker is made out of one of the
toughest materials known to man: titanium. This
allows the pen to be built all-in-one, that is to say
with an integral nib unit. The T1 was so expensive
and the technical problems encountered so intrac-
table that manufacture was discontinued less than a
year after it was marketed.

This attractive 1980s model is made of ivory. In spite of some original and often select cases (see also pages 360 and 361), the French firm of Redens unfortunately did not find its niche and quickly folded.

Now for quite another kind of valuable raw material: morta. Some 5,000 years ago, the sea that at the time extended north beyond the present-day estuary of the Loire River engulfed a vast oak forest whose remains can still be found buried beneath the peat. An artist from Brittany, Patrice Sébilo, crafts this jet-black fossilized wood into pens and pipes.

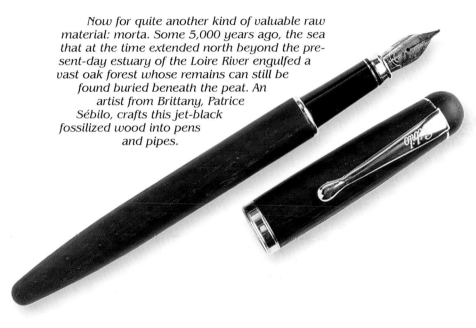

This superb pen
commemorates the
30th anniversary of the
first lunar landing, the
famous "one small step for a
man, one giant leap for man-
kind" that took place in July 1969.
This Apollo 11, by Omas, with its
white-gold-filled blue resin body, is a
worthy tribute to that event.

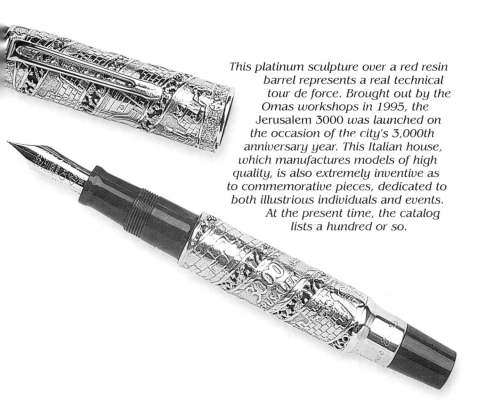

This platinum sculpture over a red resin barrel represents a real technical tour de force. Brought out by the Omas workshops in 1995, the Jerusalem 3000 was launched on the occasion of the city's 3,000th anniversary year. This Italian house, which manufactures models of high quality, is also extremely inventive as to commemorative pieces, dedicated to both illustrious individuals and events. At the present time, the catalog lists a hundred or so.

Merlin l'Enchanteur is an astonishing piece of wizardry by Michel Audiard. Judge for yourselves: the solid gold cap contains a particle of the Allende meteorite that fell into a tiny north Mexican village of the same name in 1969 and whose 4.5 billion-year-old fragments are the oldest thing on the face of the Earth. The ring is made out of a piece of another meteorite, the Gibeon, discovered in Namibia in 1836, while the barrel contains some of the Nantan that landed in 1516 and was unearthed in China in 1958...

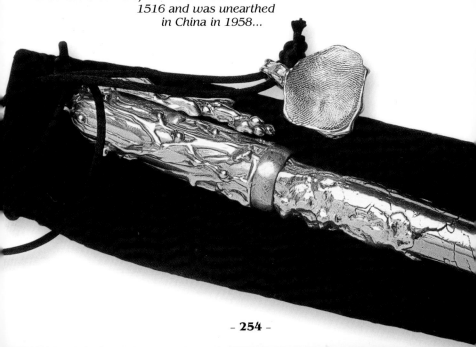

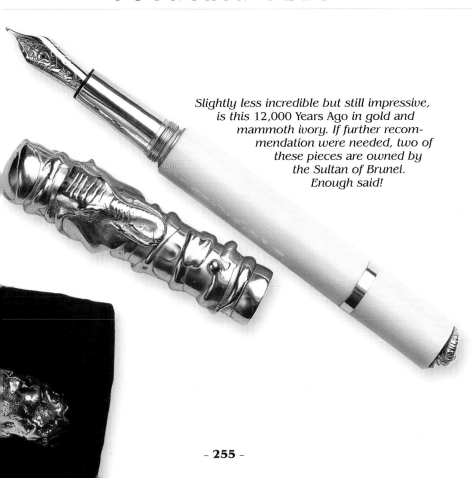

Slightly less incredible but still impressive, is this 12,000 Years Ago in gold and mammoth ivory. If further recommendation were needed, two of these pieces are owned by the Sultan of Brunel. Enough said!

The decorative pattern on these two Visconti Taj Mahals is inspired by the marquetry adorning the walls inside the world's most famous mausoleum built by Emperor Shah Jahan in the seventeenth century in honor of his young wife who died at his side during a military campaign. The one here is decorated in silver; that on the facing page, in silver-gilt. Both date from 1995.

There also exists a version
of the Taj Mahal in ivory
with gold trim. These pens
form part of a line in which
another tribute, this time to the
Grenada Alhambra, also features
(see page 304). Note the absence of
clip: the Taj Mahal is a desk pen.
Moreover, the body is designed for writing without the cap posted on the end as
this forms a complete decorative element
only when the nib is covered.

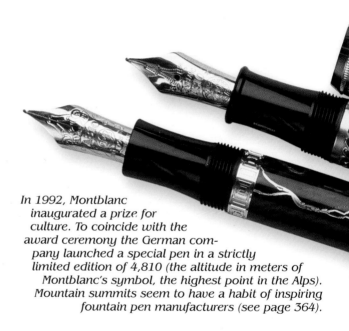

In 1992, Montblanc
inaugurated a prize for
culture. To coincide with the
award ceremony the German company launched a special pen in a strictly
limited edition of 4,810 (the altitude in meters of
Montblanc's symbol, the highest point in the Alps).
Mountain summits seem to have a habit of inspiring
fountain pen manufacturers (see page 364).

The first in a long line of pens dedicated to great patrons of the past was the Lorenzo de' Medici, created in 1992. It is quite impossible to find one today and it would be worth four times its price at launch. Shown here are a Semiramis (top) from 1996, named for the queen of Assyria and Babylon who is supposed to have planted the famous hanging gardens, and an Alexander the Great (bottom) from 1998.

1997 represents
an exceptional vintage in Montblanc's
patrons of the arts series of pens: two illustrious personages
were honored at the same, Peter the Great (by a pen in green
and his wife, Catherine I (by one in a deep red). Both were
instrumental in developing the culture of their vast country
setting up the Academy of Science, a naval academy, and an
engineering institute, as well as various organizations to
promote literature

In 1995, Montegrappa created a pen that met with considerable success: this was the Dragon with high-relief carving on a black celluloid base. Demand outstripped supply, so two years later this Italian concern decided to bring out the Luxor, in solid silver or gold over blue celluloid in a contrast full of character.

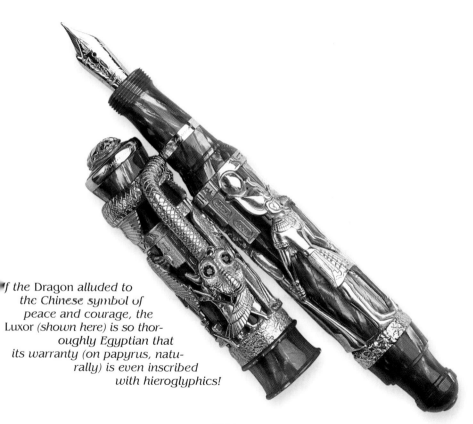

f the Dragon alluded to the Chinese symbol of peace and courage, the Luxor (shown here) is so thoroughly Egyptian that its warranty (on papyrus, naturally) is even inscribed with hieroglyphics!

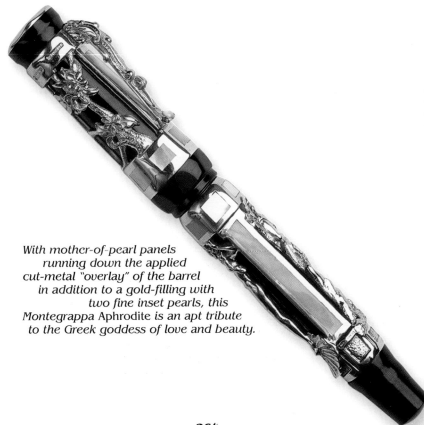

With mother-of-pearl panels
running down the applied
cut-metal "overlay" of the barrel
in addition to a gold-filling with
two fine inset pearls, this
Montegrappa Aphrodite is an apt tribute
to the Greek goddess of love and beauty.

Though it too incorporates gold and mother-of-pearl, this Parker 15 is far older than its counterpart on the page opposite that dates only from 1997. During the first decade of the twentieth century, Parker produced a number of models clad in mother-of-pearl, in particular lucky-curve system pens with fine, slender bodies. Note here the pretty filigree cap, floridly engraved with the original owner's initials: RBI.

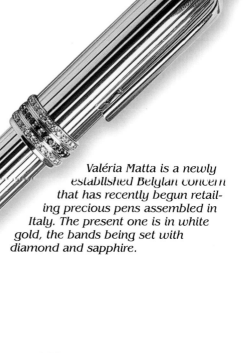

Valéria Matta is a newly established Belgian concern that has recently begun retailing precious pens assembled in Italy. The present one is in white gold, the bands being set with diamond and sapphire.

If the high price means that Valéria Matta pens are not widely available, they remain interesting products in the eyes of enthusiasts. This one, dating from 1999, is in gold braid.

Designed by a sculptor, Manou Zurini, for the
French firm of Pygmalion, this pen must
be one of the heaviest in existence,
weighing in at 3¾ oz. This model is
in silver-gilt, though titanium is
also available. Its uneven-sided
octagonal profile entails
painstaking and exact
working on the lathe
during manufacture.

The Parker make has often been associated with signing major treaties such as the antinuclear accords between Reagan and Gorbachev in 1987, the 1992 Bush–Yeltsin agreements, and the ratification of self-government for Jericho and the Gaza strip in 1993. The examples above were made for the SALT agreements signed between Bush and Gorbachev in July 1991. Generally manufactured in an edition of three to forestall mishap, such pens, rarely nibbed, are obviously not readily available to collectors. This case is preserved in the Musée International du Stylo (the international museum of the pen; see page 374).

Established in 1991, the Italian maker of this pen adopted the eminently symbolic name of Stipula as it derives from the Roman tradition of breaking a branch or straw known as a stipula, a term that lives on in the modern Italian meaning of "underwriting" a contract. Prometheus is the third in a line of strictly limited edition models based on mythological themes. These silver or gold cased pens are made using the age-old lost-wax process.

In Greek mythology, Prometheus is known as the creator of the human race and of civilization generally. He is supposed to have fashioned the first man out of clay, stealing a spark of heavenly fire to infuse his creations with life. To punish his disobedience, Zeus chained him to a great rock in the Caucasus and condemned him to having an eagle feed on his constantly regenerating liver. Prometheus was finally freed by Hercules who dispatched the dreaded eagle. See pages 306 and 307 for two other pens in the same line.

*Released in 1965, this design was among the
very earliest limited series to enjoy success, so
kicking off a fashion that has since snowballed
considerably. In an edition limited to 4,821, the
Spanish Treasure, based on the Parker 75, was
cased in part of the silver recovered from a
Spanish galleon that sank off the Florida coast on
July 31, 1715. Here in its original presentation
box—thereby greatly enhancing its value—the
actual pen sold for the eminently reasonable sum
at the time of 75 dollars. In the same vein,
Parker's Queen Elizabeth was manufactured out
of copper taken from the transatlantic liner of
the same name gutted during a fire in the
port of Hong Kong in 1972. Limited to
5,000 sets, the series hit the stores
in 1997.*

POWDER SHIP'S WATER CARGO SHIP'S
STORES   STORES   BALLAST STONES
                                 SAIL ROOM   LINE SHIP'S BOTTOM

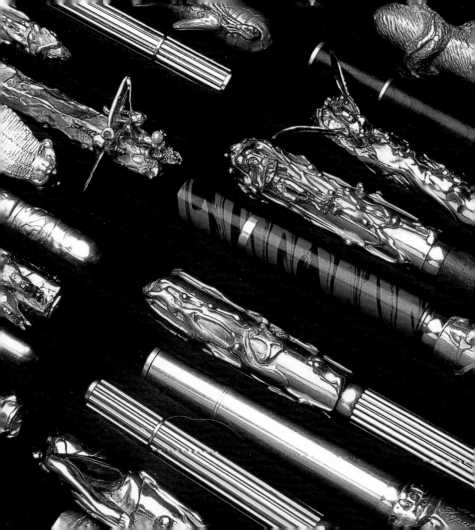

IV

THEMATIC
fountain pens

There is no shortage of fountain pens based on a theme—be it on cars, games and sport, or on the animal, vegetable or mineral worlds. There are others that on first sight look ordinary enough but that in fact commemorate some dramatic event, evoke a place of legend, or are dedicated to a famous person. Writers, naturally enough, form particularly popular subjects. On the following pages you will find a small selection that, though far from exhaustive, may give you some idea of how to start or organize your own collection. Some of the models represented are very valuable, others less so, but each has its own particular appeal, and, as in so many areas of interest, variety is the spice of life!

A very aerodynamically designed pen indeed: Omas's aluminum Ayrton Senna. Still on the automobile track, this company now turns out pens under the Ferrari name that were formerly designed by Aurora.

With its clip in the shape of a Formula One, this model is also an Ayrton Senna. With chunkier lines than the piece opposite, this 1997 Montegrappa is, however, made of a more precious material: solid silver.

Since 1995, the French sculptor Michel Audiard has been making extraordinary lost-wax method fountain pens on any number of themes. This pen, a Rêve du Mans is, until further notice, a one-off.

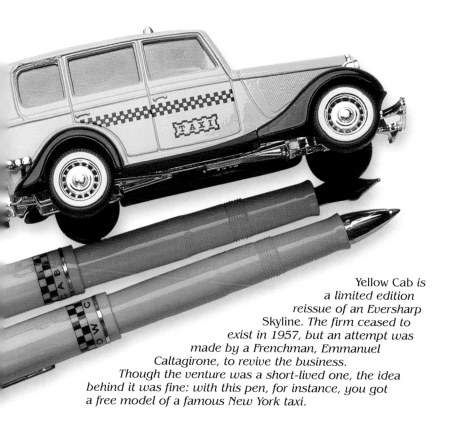

Yellow Cab *is
a limited edition
reissue of an Eversharp*
Skyline. *The firm ceased to
exist in 1957, but an attempt was
made by a Frenchman, Emmanuel
Caltagirone, to revive the business.
Though the venture was a short-lived one, the idea
behind it was fine: with this pen, for instance, you got
a free model of a famous New York taxi.*

The theme of this Waterman Gothic is games: the checkerboard pattern is gold-plated. This should not be confused with a French-made model which is called Damier ("drafts-board"). The filling system on this 1930s model is lever-operated and the body is hard rubber.

Montegrappa's Marostica derives both its name and styling from a town near Venice. In 1454, Rinaldo d'Angaramo and Vieri de Vallonora locked horns to see which of the two knights would win the right to the heart of Lionora, the daughter of the owner of Marostica Castle: to sort out their differences, however, they opted not for the sword but for the chessboard. Since then, every Friday, Saturday, and Sunday in September, Marostica's main square is an arena for an outsized game of chess in which the pieces are real-life people.

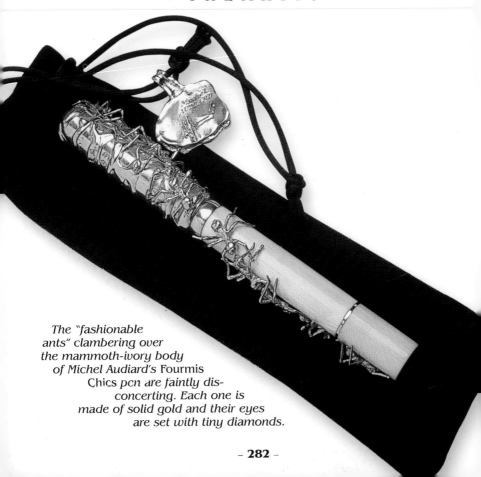

The "fashionable
ants" clambering over
the mammoth-ivory body
of Michel Audiard's Fourmis
Chics pen are faintly dis-
concerting. Each one is
made of solid gold and their eyes
are set with tiny diamonds.

This is a 1998 remake of Parker's fabled Snake pen (see page 227). Fascinated with the success of the original pen, or else perhaps with the animal itself, many suppliers have gone in for models decorated with serpents. If this theme happens to take your fancy, you'll have little difficulty in building up a collection.

Do you number among the lucky clients of the civil engineering company for whom Michel Audiard made La Pelleteuse? This "grabber-digger" pen is cased in silver-plated bronze over an ebonite body.

The same designer is also responsible for the Jambes de M pen. Whose legs are they? Madame's? Marilyn's? Or Madonna's perhaps? After all, the singer does possess a version of this gold-plated and ebony pen...

From the Italian stable of Delta, Saxo is a be-
lated pen tribute to Adolphe Saxe. The instrument maker was of course the inventor of
the saxophone, but also of the saxhorn
and even the saxotromba, a kind of
trumpet. Delta also has on the
drawing-board a pen design
intended as a homage to
the film director
Federico Fellini.

Octavian,
from the year
1993, is another,
slightly updated, re-
issue of a model from the
1920s: Montblanc's Spider.
As will be seen on the following
pages, this company is still very
active, with a host of
special lines that go down
particularly well with collectors.

In conjunction with
lines devoted to great
artistic patrons of the past,
Montblanc has also created
the Writers Edition series dedicated to
major world authors. This 1992
Hemmingway was the first.

Dated 1996, this
is the Alexandre
Dumas. There were two
writers with this name,
father and son, but it is the
elder who is celebrated here. These
are limited edition pens (see page 258),
and early lines, such as the Hemmingway
on the facing page, are today impossible to find.

A splendid trio, as much in respect of the pens themselves as the great minds they are designed to honor. But judge for yourselves. From left to right: Edgar Allan Poe (1998), Friedrich Schiller (2000), with the brown cap, and Fyodor Dostoevsky (1997). Note the range in period, country of origin, and intellectual type represented by each writer.

*And last but not least,
here is Voltaire, from 1995.
This is not even the
complete collection—there's
no forgetting Agatha Christie
(1993), and then Oscar Wilde
(1994) and, for 2001, Charles
Dickens. Writers, though, are not
Montblanc's sole source of inspiration
(see pages 258 to 261).*

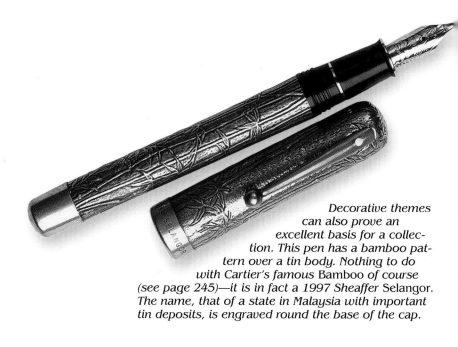

Decorative themes can also prove an excellent basis for a collection. This pen has a bamboo pattern over a tin body. Nothing to do with Cartier's famous Bamboo of course (see page 245)—it is in fact a 1997 Sheaffer Selangor. The name, that of a state in Malaysia with important tin deposits, is engraved round the base of the cap.

Hedera *is a vine-leaf design by*
Jean-Pierre Lépine, a swiss craftsman
who makes captivating
contemporary styles.
This is a 1998 edition limited
to 1,000 in plastic (rho-
doid) and
silver-gilt.

*This enchanting lady's model with ring-clip
is a solid silver Waterman dating from
around 1925. The floral and leafy case
design here is less frequent than grooved,
barleycorn, or geometric patterns.*

One of the many cases made for Waterman's CF line. Some of the finest jewelers, not the least Cartier, have tried their hand at these. The present example with a "crocodile" design dates from the end of the 1970s. there are so many different versions of the CF that it could constitute the theme for an entire collection of its own (see pages 172 to 174).

Made around 1915, this beautifully constructed no-name fountain pen was, it would appear, made to order. It is a silver eye-dropper, decorated with a set-square and a pair of compasses. These two Masonic symbols are attributes of the free man, aiding him in his quest for understanding of the external world. Is this not also one of the deeper purposes of the fountain pen itself?

A splendid Conklin in celluloid aptly christened Halloween, whose decoration
provides ample scope for the imagi-
nation to picture all manner of
ghouls and beasties. The varied
color schemes on vintage and
modern celluloid pens alike
constitute an interesting
and eye-catching theme
for a collection.

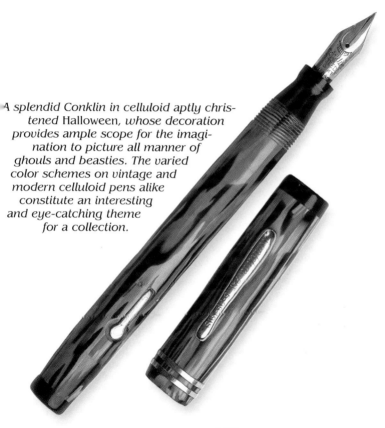

The makers of both these pens took inspiration from the 50th anniversary of the creation of the State of Israel, in 1998. The upper one is a Montegrappa studded with Stars of David and a clip adorned with a seven-branched candlestick. The one underneath is a silver Bexley model, also available in gold.

*Created for the same
occasion as the models
opposite, the Israel 50 was
made by the Italian house of
Delta. Both fountain pen and rollerball pen are made of silver, but
others exist that are gold-filled. One
of the latter, bearing the number 1948,
was presented by the makers to the
President of Israel at the time,
Ezer Weizman.*

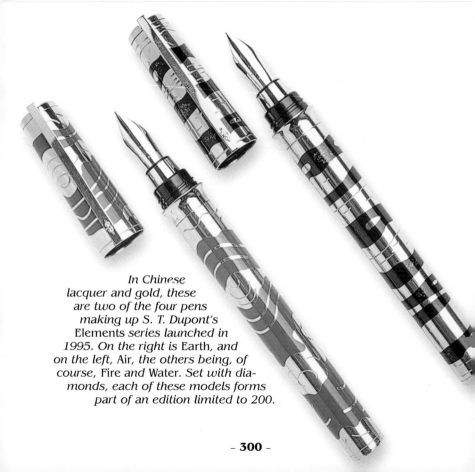

In Chinese lacquer and gold, these are two of the four pens making up S. T. Dupont's Elements series launched in 1995. On the right is Earth, and on the left, Air, the others being, of course, Fire and Water. Set with diamonds, each of these models forms part of an edition limited to 200.

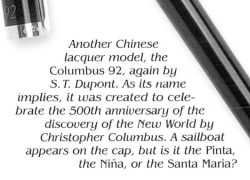

Another Chinese lacquer model, the Columbus 92, *again by S.T. Dupont. As its name implies, it was created to celebrate the 500th anniversary of the discovery of the New World by Christopher Columbus. A sailboat appears on the cap, but is it the* Pinta, *the* Niña, *or the* Santa Maria?

This
Sheaffer is a
Balance, a model
we have already encountered
on pages 100 and 101. This specimen is rather original, however, in
that the cap-band is wide enough to be
engraved with the owner's name.
A collection that concentrates systematically
on personalized models—be they pre-owned by
celebs (see facing page) or by less famous individuals—should lead to the unearthing of some
fantastic models.

*This pen, with
its exceptionally pure lines is
remarkable from more than one
point of view. It was given as a present to the famous aviator Jacqueline
Auriol by one of her many admirers,
Jacqueline Cockran, the first woman to go
through the sound barrier. Moreover, the basic
pen is by Sheaffer but the case is a Cartier. Donated
by Jean-Pierre Philibert, it belongs to the Musée
International du Stylo (address page 374).*

Launched in 1995 by Visconti, the Alhambra is one of the most interesting modern fountain pens. Its decoration has been embedded using a niello-like technique (see page 310) that is rendered still more complicated here since the fine-silver filigree overlay is in very slight relief. The pattern itself is an elaborate one and also features a groove running along the motif. Both the hard rubber barrel and cap are in red, a hue particularly difficult to obtain in this material as it corresponds to a specific mid-stage in its production. A few dozen examples of this model exist with gold filigree and trim.

One of Visconti's more remarkable lines is the Camelot, *the name of the legendary city of King Arthur and his Knights of the Round Table. The clip is a stylized sword, while the pen is clad without visible joins with a pattern resembling chain-mail. This model, from 1998, is in fine red ebonite.*

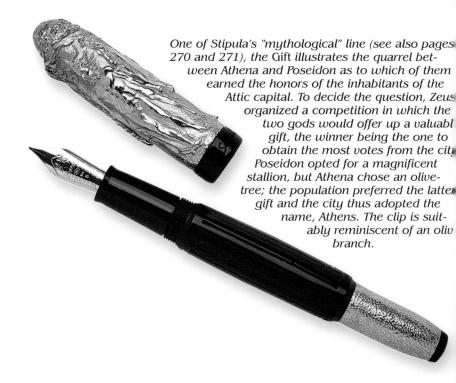

One of Stipula's "mythological" line (see also pages 270 and 271), the Gift illustrates the quarrel between Athena and Poseidon as to which of them earned the honors of the inhabitants of the Attic capital. To decide the question, Zeus organized a competition in which the two gods would offer up a valuabl gift, the winner being the one to obtain the most votes from the cit Poseidon opted for a magnificent stallion, but Athena chose an olive-tree; the population preferred the latter gift and the city thus adopted the name, Athens. The clip is suitably reminiscent of an oliv branch.

Ulysses' dog Argus was the only one to recognize the wandering hero on his return to Ithaca disguised in a beggar's rags, though at the sight he died of joy. His exemplary fidelity is illustrated on this Stipula model; the carving is the work of the Florentine sculptor Paolo Cerrini.

Among the most recent
Stipula limited edition models,
these Academia pens bear emblems referring
to three outdoor pursuits: polo, golf, and angling. Like all
the special edition models by this maker,
they are piston fillers.

Herewith the myth of Icarus as imagined by Pelikan—for once leaving off its celebrated black and green color scheme. Even as we enter the third millennium, mythology appears to remain the height of fashion! In an edition limited to 800, Icarus is another piston filler.

Jointly with Pilot-Namiki and Platinum, Sailor is one of the three largest Japanese pen manufacturers. The 1976 Hieroglyphic model shown here is a limited edition. It is in a sterling silver niello that is made by pouring black enamel composition into the intaglio parts of the engraved design.

The firm of Krone, which otherwise manufactures thoroughbred classical lines, does not flinch from the spectacular for its special series. Space in Time is clad with a lacquer landscape painted by a Russian artist over mother-of-pearl. This impressive Neo-Classical model came out in 2001.

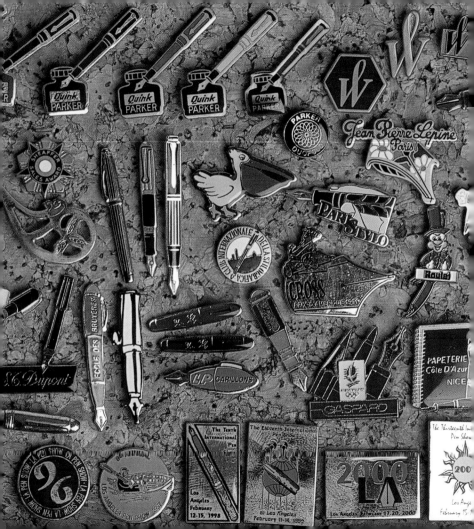

V

UNUSUAL
fountain pens

Appearances can be deceptive: in the bottom of a dusty old box in the attic there lies an assortment of discarded objects including a fountain pen. You pick it up, take off the cap, inspect it, and hey presto! It turns out not to be a pen at all but a razor, or a corkscrew, or a penknife. For lovers of gadgets, there are also models that write as genuine pens, but cleverly double up as thermometers, watches or cigarette lighters. Then there exist fountain pens clad in unexpected materials, sometimes precious, sometimes not. In short, there exists a wealth of curious pens that collectors just can't resist amassing and presenting alongside the more traditional models.

Demonstration models are one of the curiosities of the pen world. The one illustrated is a Sheaffer Balance from the end of the 1920s. Naturally, such models are manufactured in far smaller numbers than "real" pens destined for the market and are not easy to find in a good state of preservation, above all when the model itself was successful!

A Parker 51 demonstration model with a Vacumatic filling system. The plunger activates a diaphragm that creates a vacuum to suck up the ink into the pen. If the Parker 51 happens to be one your favorite collectibles you should try to get your hands on a demonstration model of the Aeromatic that replaced the Vacumatic in 1947.

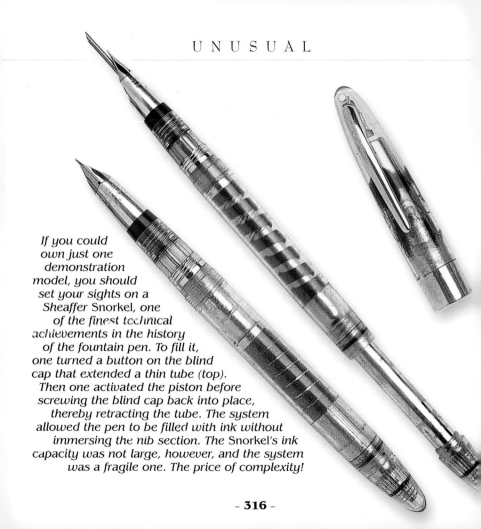

*If you could
own just one
demonstration
model, you should
set your sights on a
Sheaffer Snorkel, one
of the finest technical
achievements in the history
of the fountain pen. To fill it,
one turned a button on the blind
cap that extended a thin tube (top).
Then one activated the piston before
screwing the blind cap back into place,
thereby retracting the tube. The system
allowed the pen to be filled with ink without
immersing the nib section. The Snorkel's ink
capacity was not large, however, and the system
was a fragile one. The price of complexity!*

This *Extra*
361 by Omas,
quite apart from being a
superb celluloid example, possesses a
peculiar feature: the nib can be used on
both sides, each offering a different degree
of flexibility and thickness. It was nicknamed
the "million dollar pen," not after its price of
course but because this was the amount offered to
the founder of Omas, Armando Simoni, to surrender
the patent. He refused, naturally enough!

What a clever idea: two nibs with different color inks in the same pen! This was especially useful in an age when the keeping of handwritten accounts called for entries in red and black (or violet) ink on every page. This pen uses a system of retractable nibs: when one goes into the barrel, the other comes out. The photograph here shows them in the process of switching, hence both can be seen peeking out simultaneously.

Another two-color ink system: Colorado by Omas. This model comprises twin "half pens" on a pair of metal plates held together by a hinge. The cap can be posted only when the two nibs lie face to face, whereas, in use, they are at opposite ends. The little dots—red on one end and black on the other—indicate the ink color. This pen started in production in 1948 and was on the market for about a decade.

These are two examples of wha collectors term security pens Patented by the firm of Kritikso Brothers, Chicago, the pen wa designed to enhance check secu rity. Once the amount on the check had been filled in, a whee in the pen's cap top could be rolled over it ..

.. thereby rendering later altera-
ion impossible. The patent was
odged on May 4, 1920, and, between 1924 and 1928, models
vere made and sold by students
at Lincoln College, Indiana, to
partly finance their studies! Note
the distinctive marbling on these
two hard-rubber models.

Although the idea seemed a reasonable one in theory, adjustable nibs never really caught on in practice. The sticking point was that, once the customer had chosen a point perfectly suited to their handwriting in the store, being able to alter the nib's flexibility afterwards was only of marginal interest. This is a 1979 Pilot Adjustas. The nib is adjusted from underneath.

On this Eversharp Coronet, which came out in 1936, the nib is adjusted by means of a slide: the closer it is moved toward the tip, the harder the point, and vice versa. On more recent models the slide is not cut away, as here, but a solid piece. This nib system was, however, delicate in use and costly to produce.

Brought out by the French makers
La Plume d'Or in 1932, the Pullman
includes an intriguing feature:
depressing a button at the end of
the pen with one hand opens a
hinged cover through which
the nib emerges; and the
same action retracts it
back into the body

The Pullman *possesses no independent cap since it forms an integral part of the barrel. In addition, when the pen is open in the writing position, the cover can be used as a rest for the index or middle finger under the nib. This button-filler model also exists in black hard rubber (as here) and marble.*

The two Watermans here were intended for the very specific task of taking shorthand. The long body could store a considerable quantity of ink and thus save one from frequently having to refill the pen during dictation. The pen at the top is fitted with a retractable nib. The other one is a regular eyedropper filler.

Invented by Alonzo Townsend Cross around 1876, this Stylographic Pen *ushered in a revolution in the practice of business correspondence. Instead of bearing a flexible nib, it was fitted with a strong tubular needle that exerted sufficient pressure to make multiple carbon copies. This rare model is the ancestor of the* Rapidograph *by the* German company of Rotring who specialize in technical drawing instruments.

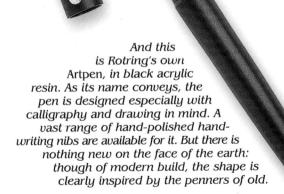

And this
is Rotring's own
Artpen, in black acrylic
resin. As its name conveys, the
pen is designed especially with
calligraphy and drawing in mind. A
vast range of hand-polished handwriting nibs are available for it. But there is
nothing new on the face of the earth:
though of modern build, the shape is
clearly inspired by the penners of old.

Reform, a German maker, is a favorite with calligraphers. The nib of this Calligraphic is, like all pens dedicated to the art, cut straight, without a point. After a bit of practice holding the pen in the correct position, one can soon produce beautiful up- and down-strokes both thin and thick.

This 1920s lady's Waterman is fitted with two caps that can be posted over either end of the barrel. One, with a cap-ring, could be hung on a little chain and remain there; and the spare cap could still serve to close the pen if one wanted to leave it on one's desk.

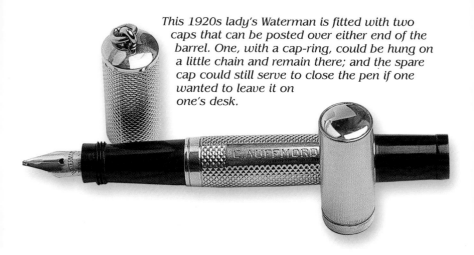

This is a strange beast, a pen concealing a stamp in the barrel. This kind of gadget made it possible to leave one's personal details on any piece of paper to hand. Pens like this German Goldrin were the acme of fashion in the 1960s.

Made by the
English company of
Balmain (no connection
with the famous French
couturier), this pen contains
a roll of blotting-paper
wrapped round a hinged axle
that can be turned and wheeled
over the wet ink.

Still with direct applications in the world of correspondence, this model is an American-designed letter balance. The body is marbled plastic and, like its counterpart opposite, dates from the 1930s.

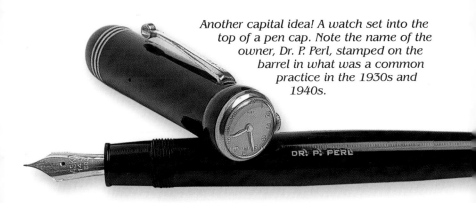

Another capital idea! A watch set into the top of a pen cap. Note the name of the owner, Dr. P. Perl, stamped on the barrel in what was a common practice in the 1930s and 1940s.

Cartier has long
proposed models incorporating
timekeepers, following the same principle as
the watch on the facing page, but they are mainly ball-
points or mechanical pencils. Fountain pens combined
with a calendar are also a classic style of this maker. The
one shown above in its original presentation box is solid
gold and dates from the 1920s.

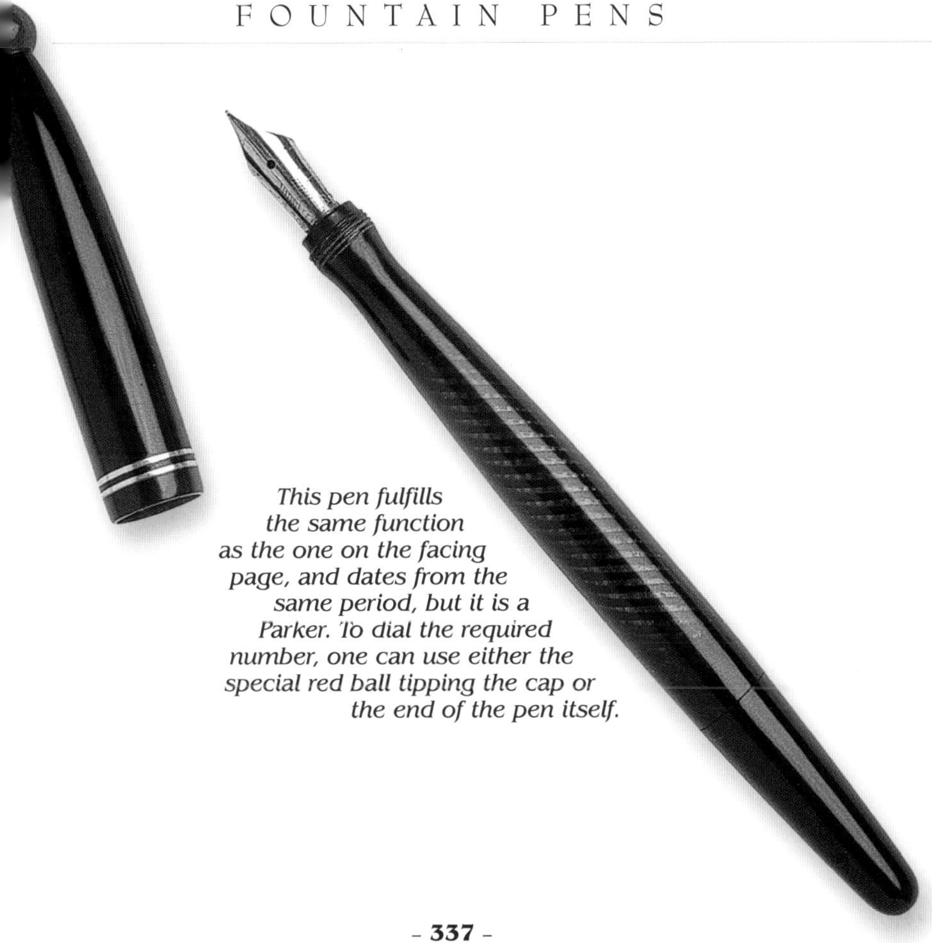

This pen fulfills the same function as the one on the facing page, and dates from the same period, but it is a Parker. To dial the required number, one can use either the special red ball tipping the cap or the end of the pen itself.

Two extremes: the biggest and the tiniest pens known. The first is a Pilot-Namiki Emperor in vermilion lacquer, 6¾ inches long and still being manufactured. As for the latter, the Waterman Doll Pen dates from 1910 and measures just over 1½ inches!

The Doll Pen *was a real technological tour de force as it functions exactly like a normal-sized pen. Here it is reproduced at approximately twice its actual size.*

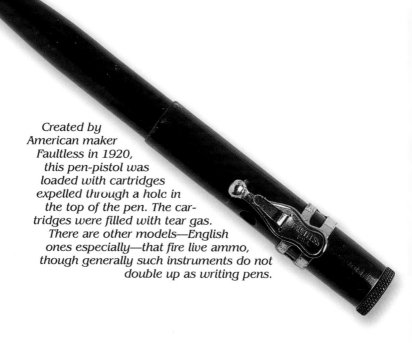

Created by
American maker
Faultless in 1920,
this pen-pistol was
loaded with cartridges
expelled through a hole in
the top of the pen. The cartridges were filled with tear gas.
There are other models—English
ones especially—that fire live ammo,
though generally such instruments do not
double up as writing pens.

*This is a
1932* Holy Water
Dispenser *pen by
Chilton: just press the plunger, and out
it comes! Waterman, Parker, and Le Bœuf
launched similar models in the 1920s.*

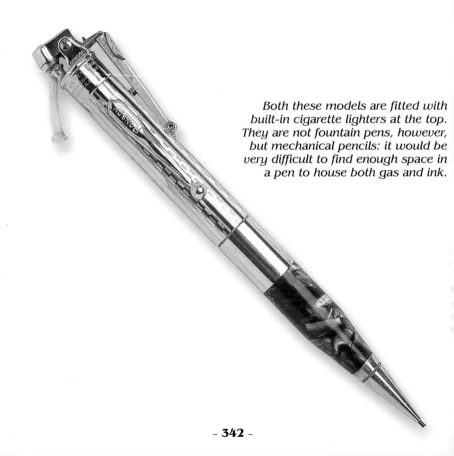

Both these models are fitted with built-in cigarette lighters at the top. They are not fountain pens, however, but mechanical pencils: it would be very difficult to find enough space in a pen to house both gas and ink.

They work rather differently too: in the recent model on the left, it is the clip that fires the spark. The vintage model above has an old-fashioned wheel that has to be turned to light the wick.

UNUSUAL

Sheaffer has always stood at the forefront of innovation. In 1933, it launched the Telephone Dialer, a pen whose pointed rather than smooth end could be inserted into old-style, round dialers and rotated to dial the number. (Much kinder on the fingernails!)

*With the
cap on, this
looks like a common-
or-garden black hard-rubber
pen. In fact, it's a razor—one that
shaves rather well what's more.
Dating from 1910, it was made by
the firm of Arnold's.*

*This model is
another technical mar-
vel: a thermometer housed in the body
of a pen that otherwise functions in the
normal manner. From 1900, it was made by
the Detroit-based Laughlin company which manufactured some superb models.*

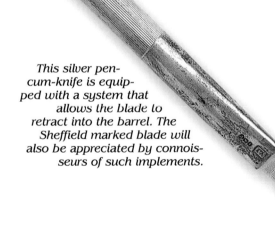

This silver pen-cum-knife is equipped with a system that allows the blade to retract into the barrel. The Sheffield marked blade will also be appreciated by connoisseurs of such implements.

This amusing little propelling pencil also contains a complete manicure set: cuticle pen, nail files, and cutter are all of high quality and, although they are hinged together, easy to use. A more difficult task is to get the contraption back into the barrel, which, fully closed, once again looks like a fountain pen.

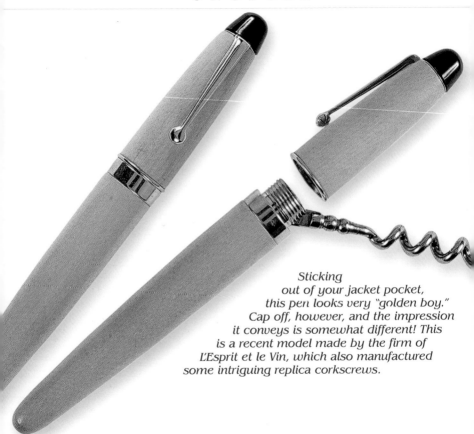

*Sticking
out of your jacket pocket,
this pen looks very "golden boy."
Cap off, however, and the impression
it conveys is somewhat different! This
is a recent model made by the firm of
L'Esprit et le Vin, which also manufactured
some intriguing replica corkscrews.*

This little charmer
is the perfect partner for the "pen" oppo-
site: a pretty model in the shape of a wine bot-
tle. To start writing, one screws the nib unit onto
the "barrel," which then turns into a normal size
fountain pen. The unit fits snugly in the
barrel when not in use.

This rollerball is more a gag than anything else.
Dating from the 1990s, its name means "crib" and
the purpose of the piece of paper is all too
obvious. Joke though it may be, examina-
tion invigilators may take less
than kindly to its use in
the field!

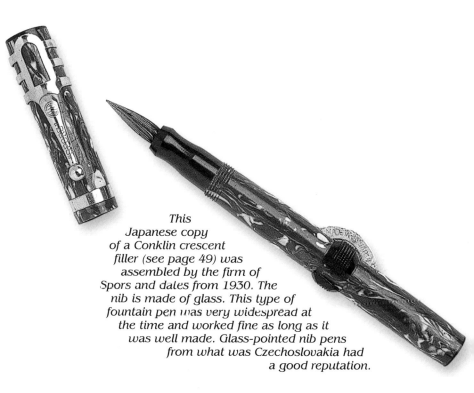

*This
Japanese copy
of a Conklin crescent
filler (see page 49) was
assembled by the firm of
Spors and dates from 1930. The
nib is made of glass. This type of
fountain pen was very widespread at
the time and worked fine as long as it
was well made. Glass-pointed nib pens
from what was Czechoslovakia had
a good reputation.*

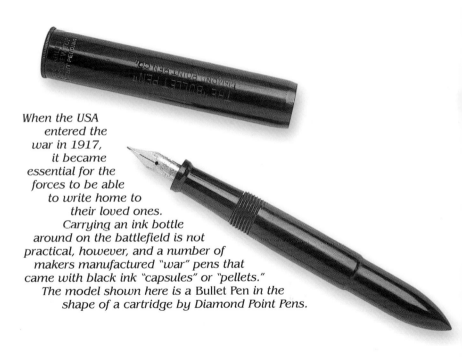

When the USA
entered the
war in 1917,
it became
essential for the
forces to be able
to write home to
their loved ones.
Carrying an ink bottle
around on the battlefield is not
practical, however, and a number of
makers manufactured "war" pens that
came with black ink "capsules" or "pellets."
The model shown here is a Bullet Pen in the
shape of a cartridge by Diamond Point Pens.

As
for this
one, it's a
"trench" pen,
Mabie Todd's Military
No. 2. *Both models carry the dissolving
ink capsule in a compartment housed
within the blind cap, clearly visible here,
and date from 1917.*

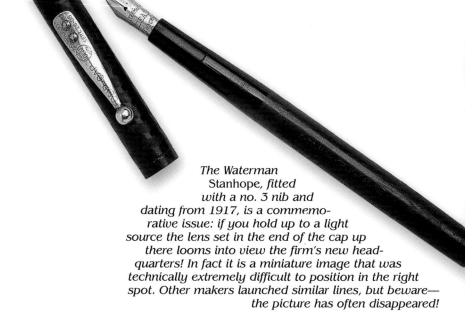

The Waterman
Stanhope, *fitted*
with a no. 3 nib and
dating from 1917, is a commemo-
rative issue: if you hold up to a light
source the lens set in the end of the cap up
there looms into view the firm's new head-
quarters! In fact it is a miniature image that was
technically extremely difficult to position in the right
spot. Other makers launched similar lines, but beware—
the picture has often disappeared!

The
image on
offer here is alto-
gether more titillating,
the lens on the cap top containing
a picture of a scantily clad young
woman lounging on a sofa. Otherwise,
this pen, in black hard rubber, looks
positively sober...

Three porcelain-styled pens: Lady models, by Lamy, which, belying its name, is actually a German company with headquarters in Heidelberg. These pens were manufactured with the assistance of the porcelain factory, Rosenthal. The style concept is by an Indonesian artist, Yang, while designer Wolfgang Fabian is responsible for the form. The pen on this page came out in 1999 and the one opposite in 1994.

One can see that none of these pens has a clip, but are fitted instead with two little buttons, one on the cap and the other on the barrel, to prevent the pen rolling. Such models—in common with all Lamy's high-end styles—sell like hot cakes to lovers of contemporary design.

*This elegant
ladies' Waterman is
adorned with eggshell
inlay of the same type as
that found on pill or snuff boxes
and even on select lighters.*

This pen has the same eggshell decoration but was crafted by S.T. Dupont, a concern founded in 1872 and with a reputation for luxury leather goods and cigarette lighters. It began retailing fountain pens only in 1973 (see also pages 300 and 301).

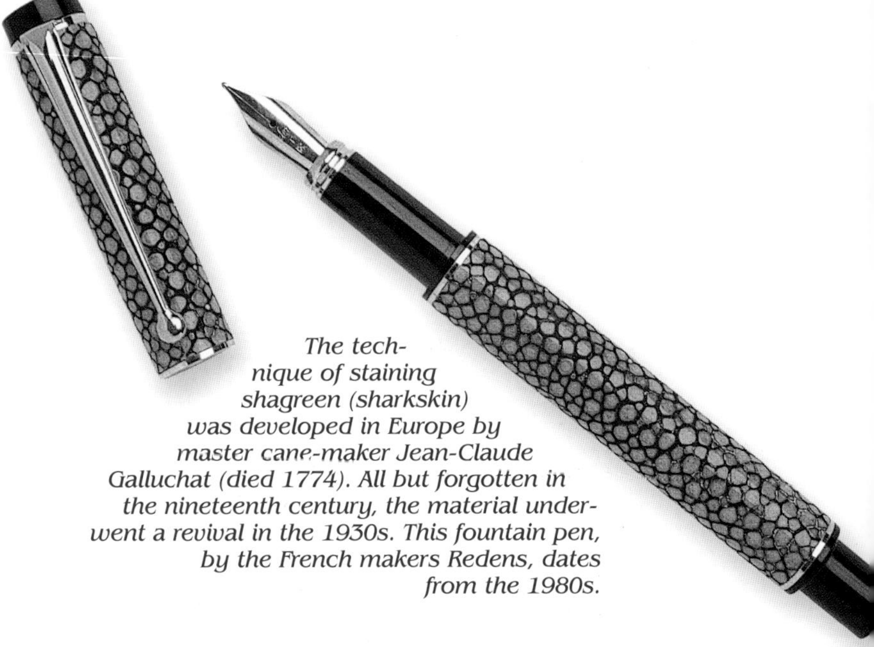

The tech-
nique of staining
shagreen (sharkskin)
was developed in Europe by
master cane-maker Jean-Claude
Galluchat (died 1774). All but forgotten in
the nineteenth century, the material underwent a revival in the 1930s. This fountain pen,
by the French makers Redens, dates
from the 1980s.

This model
is covered in
ostrich hide, and
there also exists an-
other of identical shape in
python skin. Established in
1980, the Redens mark only
remained in business for fifteen
years or so, but its models, overpriced
and at odds with the spirit of the times,
are now highly prized by collectors of
pens in novel materials.

The firm of
Platinum started life as an importer of models
from the West in the 1920s, but has since become a major Japanese manufacturer of quality
pens. In the years 1960–70, it launched a number of
leather-cased models called Amazonas, of which this is
an example clad in the skin of a Surinam toad.

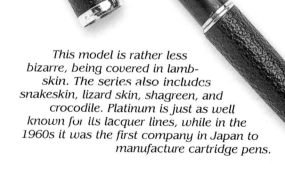

This model is rather less bizarre, being covered in lamb-skin. The series also includes snakeskin, lizard skin, shagreen, and crocodile. Platinum is just as well known for its lacquer lines, while in the 1960s it was the first company in Japan to manufacture cartridge pens.

This Platinum is covered
in woven silk. The same
makers also made the
renowned 3776 (so called after
the height of Mount Fuji in
meters), available in an extensive
range of finishes including light briar
and sandblasted briar.

After nigh on 400 pages of fountain pens and to bring us back to earth, we just cannot resist the Corgi *pen—the only furry writing instrument known to man!*

Index, Addresses & Acknowledgments

Index

The index covers proper names, makers, manufactures, and fountain pen model
quoted and/or illustrated.

INDEX

INDEX

INDEX

INDEX

INDEX

Addresses

United States

Pen Collectors of America
P.O.Box 447
Fort Madison, IA 52627-0447
Tel: 914 769 0310.
E-mail:info@pencollectors.com

Fountain Pen Hospital
10 Warren Street
New York, NY 10007
Tel: 212 964 0580
E-mail info@fountainpenhospital.com
www.fountainpenhospital.com

Arthur Brown & Bro. International
2 West 46th Street
New York, NY 10036
Tel: 800 772-PENS
E-mail: penshop@artbrown.com
www.artbrown.com

Sotheby's
1334, York Avenue
New York, NY 10021
Tel: 212 606 7000
Contact: Collectibles department

Great Britain

Christie's
85, Old Brompton Road
London SW7 3LD
Tel: 0207 581 7611
www.christies.com

Penfriend
34, Burlington Arcade
Piccadilly
London W1J 0QA
Tel: 0207 499 6337
E-mail: pen.london@btinternet.com
www.penfriend.co.uk

The Writing Equipment Society
E-mail: wes-sec@btinternet.com
www.wesoc.co.uk

France

Musée international du Stylo
3, rue Guy-de-Maupassant
75116 Paris
(The museum is open Sundays, from
2 p.m. to 6 p.m.)

Other Web sites

www.cartier.com
www.dupontpens.com
www.fountainpens.com
www.montblanc.com
www.novelli.it
www.parker-pens.com
www.pelikan.de
www.penbid.com
www.pencollectors.com
www.pendemonium.com
www.penlovers.com
www.penshop.co.uk
www.penslimited.com
www.penworld.com
www.sheaffer.com
www.stipulausa.com
www.swisherpens.com
www.waterman-pens.com
www.worldpen.com

Acknowledgments

Thanks to the following collectors for the loan of some of their most valuable models: Raymondo Ascer, Bernard Bernolet, Jean-Elie Betat, Patrice Caron, Emmanuel Feyt, Bruno Lussato, Stéphan Magnani, André Mora, Thierry Nguyen, as well as the Dubois-Vutera company.

Stop Press

As we were putting the final touches to the French edition of this book, we heard the distressing news that the whole collection of the Musée International du Stylo had been stolen. The events took place on June 22, 2001 on the museum's premises in the 16th arrondissement in Paris. Among the pens purloined were a number of priceless pieces. Since quite a few feature in this book (see list below), we make a general appeal for any information regarding their whereabouts. If you come across one of these models, please contact the Musée International du Stylo whose address can be found on page 374 or send a fax to +33 [0]1 47 20 56 26.

All models formerly in the collection together with the museum's inventory numbers:

p. 36, 426; p. 37, 427; p. 38, 440; p. 39, 435; pp. 40–41, 241; p. 42, 344; p. 43, 430; p. 44, 186; p. 45, 664; p. 48, 279; p. 49, 423; pp. 50–51, 626; p. 54, 445; p. 55, 236; p. 57, 434; p. 64, 282; p. 66, 17; p. 67, 117; p. 70, 306; p. 71, 12 and 13; p. 72, 439 (blue), 205 (olive); p. 73, 464; p. 74, 289; p. 75, 250 and 303; p. 76, 459; p. 77, 302; p. 79, 323; p. 93, 491; p. 94, 256 and 490; p. 95, 304; p. 96, 252 (Moss Agate); p. 97, 203; p. 98, 252; p. 102, 380; p. 104, 469 (black and pearl) and 369 (Cathay); p. 105, 350; p. 106, 386; p. 107, 428; p. 108, 135; p. 110, 554; p. 111, 275; p. 112, 275; p. 113, 333; p. 114, 238; p. 116, 417; p. 117, 334; p. 119, 185; p. 128, 255; p. 129, 620; p. 131, 482; p. 132, 480; p. 136, 496; p. 138, 208; p. 139, 625; p. 141, 373; p. 143, 262; p. 144, 113; p. 145, 84; p. 146, 300; p. 147, 183; p. 150, 242; p. 151, 112; p. 154, 40; p. 155, 691; pp. 156–57, 119; p. 168, 222; p. 169, 259; p. 170, 506; p. 175, 151; p. 178, 305; p. 179, 98; p. 183, 93; p. 187, 271; pp. 190–91, P.A 62—1995; p. 194, Art 92 V3—1994; p. 207, V 50 Art. 171; p. 218, 178; p. 222, 3; p. 223, 433; p. 227, 449; p. 229, 366; p. 238, N 1; p. 240, 523; p. 242, 534 and 63; p. 244, Art 147; p. 245, 619 and 477; p. 246, OM 41; p. 247, Art 23; p. 248, MB 42; p. 249, 156; p. 252, OM 166; p. 253, OM 125; p. 268, Art 136; p. 269, P.A 3; pp. 270–71, Art 154; pp. 272–73, 581; p. 276, OM 165; p. 300, D.P. 21 and D.P. 22; p. 301, D.P. 27; p. 302, 134; p. 303, 602; p. 304, Art 98 V9; p. 305, Art 168; p. 306, Art 55; p. 307, Art 178; p. 310, 132; p. 316, 310; p. 317, 337; p. 319, 546; p. 320, 489; p. 322, N19; p. 323, 78; pp. 326–27 (above), 338 and 233; p. 328, Com 2; p. 329, Com 1; p. 331, 558; p. 332, 379; p. 333, 326; p. 335, 476; p. 337, 564; p. 340, 218; p. 341, 451; p. 342, GD 63; p. 343, GD 64; p. 344, 354; p. 345, 450; p. 346, GD 67; p. 347, GD 68; p. 350, GD 69; p. 351, 36; p. 352, 314; p. 353, 173; p. 354, 321; p. 355, 628; p. 357, L7 and L8; p. 359, D.P. 2; p. 360, Art 133; p. 361, Art 137; p. 362, 122; p. 363, 87; p. 364, 216. *The exceptional pieces on pages 12, 17, 19, 21, 22 and 27 also come from the Museum's Collections.*

Bibliography

Bernard Bernolet and Marc Van der Stricht, The List,
Nivelles: Havaux, 1999.

Éric Le Collen, Objets d'écriture,
Paris: Flammarion, 1998.

A. Crum Ewing, The Fountain Pen. A Collector's Companion,
London: Apple, 1997.

G. Dragoni and G. Fichera (eds.), Fountain Pens. History and Design,
Woodbridge: Antique Collectors Club, 1998.

George Fischler and Stuart Schneider, Fountain Pens and Pencils,
Lancaster, Pa: Schiffer Publishing Ltd., 1998.

Andreas Lambrou, Fountain Pens Vintage and Modern,
London: Sotheby's, 1989.

Andreas Lambrou, Fountain Pens of the World,
Woodbridge: Antique Collectors Club, 1995

Andreas Lambrou, Fountain Pens: United States of America
and United Kingdom
Los Angeles: Classic Pens Inc., 2000.

Jonathan Steinberg, Fountain Pens,
London: Apple, 1995.

Jonathan Steinberg, Fountain Pen Identifier,
London: Apple, 1994.

In the same series

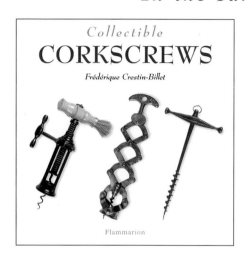

Collectible Corkscrews
by Frédérique Crestin-Billet

Collectible Pocket Knives
by Dominique Pascal

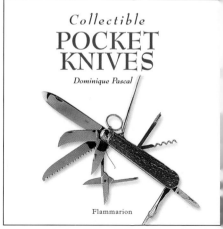

*Collectible Miniature
Perfume Bottles*
by Anne Breton

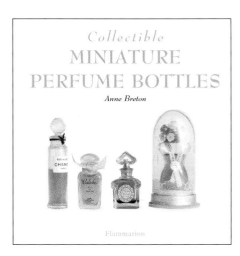

Collectible Wristwatches
by René Pannier

Photographic credits

All color photos are by Antoine Pascal,
Dominique Pascal and Olivier Renard
and come from
Archives & Collections
e–mail: archives.collections@wanadoo.fr
Copyright reserved for all other documents

FA0719-02-II
Dépôt légal: 4/2002